算盘珍藏

陈宝定　陈沅沅　著

立信会计出版社

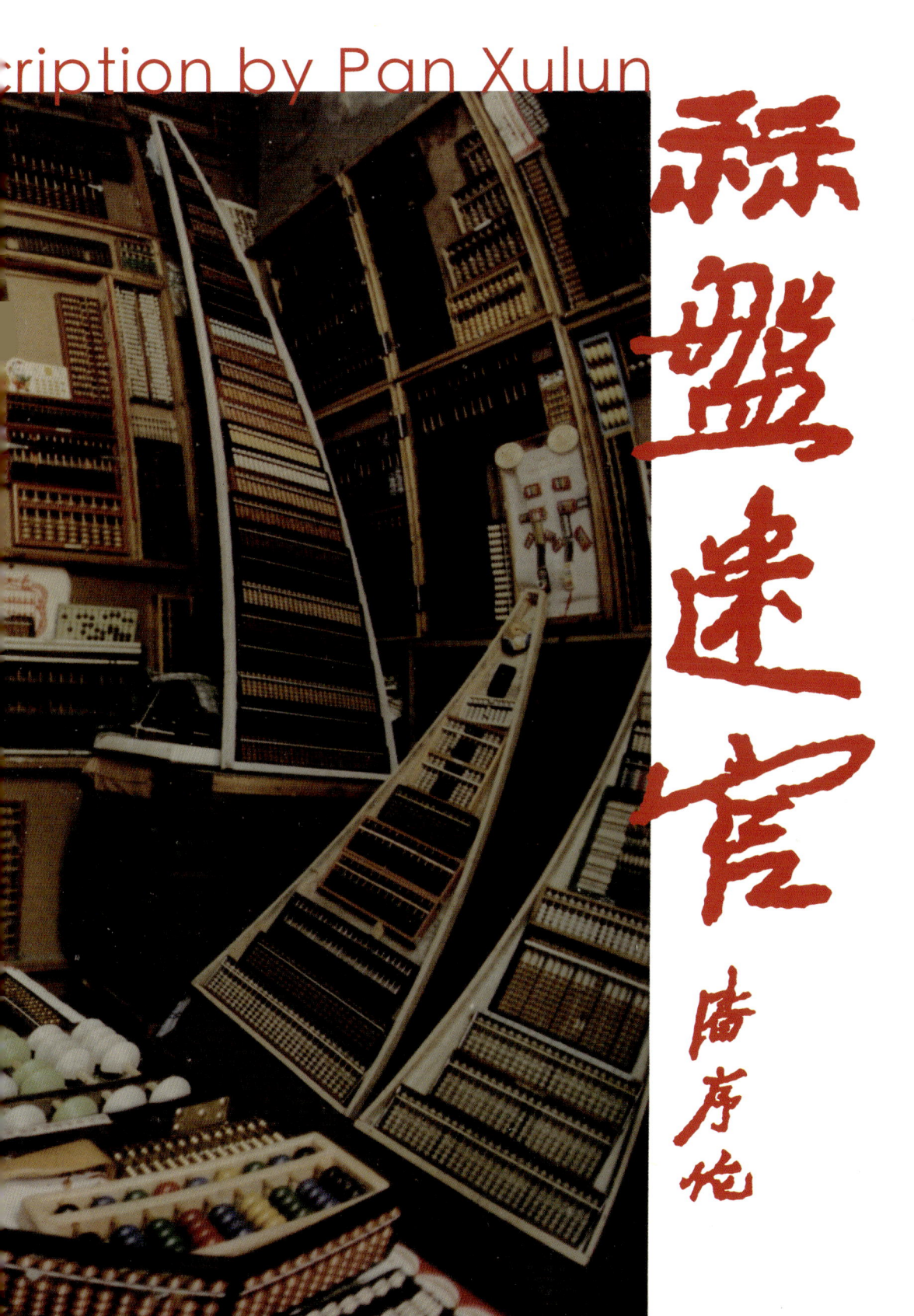

算盘述窋

潘序伦

Preface

My father, Chen Baoding, has been devoting his whole life to accounting education and abacus collection. He bimanual calculated on abacus when he was very young, since then, he showed a strong preference on it.

Throughout my father's life, he was diligent and thrifty, whereas he spent almost all his time, efforts and money on abacus collection, passing on the essence of ancient culture. In order to share this treasure, my father set up China's first abacus showroom and exhibited hundreds of abaci both ancient and modern in 1981. This showroom attracted tens of thousands of Chinese and foreign enthusiasts. Chinese "Accounting Father", Pan Xulun, was also shocked here, and called it "abacus labyrinth".

Here we edit more than 100 pieces of selected pictures into an album, not only to give a Chinese abacus history baptism, but also to further spread traditional Chinese culture. These are my father's long-cherished wish. In 2008, my father planed this album in his sick bed, however, he did not wait to see its publish.

On this occasion, I would like to acknowledge all the leaderships, editors, designers, and all the other staffs related in Shanghai Lixin University of Commerce and Lixin Accounting Publishing House for their painstaking efforts. Especially, I acknowledge the leaderships and members of Shanghai Collection Association, Chinese Abacus Association and Shou Cang magazine. And also, I acknowledge Nantong Chinese Abacus Museum for its ebullient support. The articles in this book marked as "▲" is now displaying at the Museum on the second floor.

On account of lack of time and knowledge limitation, the album may in the omission, please enlighten and correct me!

Chen Yuanyuan
December, 2009

前　言

　　"一生育才留典范，半世收藏传嘉风"是父亲陈宝定的人生轨迹。或许少年就会双手打算盘，毕生从事财会教育的父亲，一生笃爱算盘，与算盘有一种特殊的情愫。

　　半世纪以来，他为此殚精竭虑，宵衣旰食，几乎把所有的时间、精力、财力耗尽在算盘的收藏中，沉浸执著地守护、传承着这份古老文化的余脉。为了让更多的人分享、延绵中华民族的瑰宝，1981年，父亲创立国内第一间家庭算盘陈列室，将珍藏的几百件古今中外算盘展示出来。当享有"会计之父"名誉的潘序伦先生走进这座算盘宫殿时，叹为观止，当场题字"算盘迷宫"。正是这间公益性的陈列室接待了几万名中外算盘爱好者，接受了全国各地及美、日、英、法等世界各国的新闻媒体采访，影响之卓越，传播之恒久，是不言而喻的。

　　"收藏有道，藏之有方"。父亲的收藏境界与理念健康而高雅。其折射出几个特点：以藏会友；以藏促研；以藏为载体；以藏为窗口。被尊称为"海派收藏一代的楷模"。

　　遴选一百多件精品，编著成一本画册，既是对中国算盘发展史进行一次洗礼，也是中华传统文化的深度传递，这是父亲多年的夙愿。2008年在病榻上的父亲，策划了本画册的思路，但未等画册出版就谢世了，实在令人悲惋。

　　值此画册出版之际，衷心感谢上海立信会计学院和立信会计出版社领导、编辑、设计等人员付出的心血，特别感激中国珠算协会、上海收藏协会、西安《收藏》杂志领导、藏友们关心，真诚感谢南通中国算盘博物馆的全力支持。凡本画册作"▲"符号藏品，现均在该馆二楼展示。

　　由于本人学识与水平有限，时间仓促，画册中疏漏之处，敬请赐教与指正！

陈沅沅

2009年12月

Contents

目 录

第一部分 中国实用算盘

Abacus is a record of history and a special carrier of civilization.

The Chinese abacus is a great creation by ancient working people. It has more than two thousand years of history. According to the research, the Chinese abacus originated from the Tang and Song Dynasty, flourished in Yuan and Ming Dynasty. The Chinese abacus consists of four parts: deck, beam, rods and beads. Its greatest characteristic is that it has a beam and its bead on the top cover for five. The Chinese abacus is regarded as the world's oldest and most facilitated calculator.

This section shows 60 Chinese abaci, which bring together the essence of the traditional Chinese practical abacus. According to the bead shape, there are: large circular abacus, medium-sized disc abacus, mini rhombus abacus, etc.; according to the structure, there are: general abacus, folding abacus, non-rod abacus, winding-up abacus, position-setting abacus, display abacus, etc.; according to the material, there are: rosewood abacus, ivory abacus, white marble abacus, gold abacus, silver abacus, horn abacus, jade abacus and so on.

Chinese abacus embodies the wisdom and civilization of our ancestors and carries the essence of oriental nation's outstanding culture. Also, it reflects the level of our abacus achievements.

Appreciating the Chinese abacus and you'll touch the traditional Chinese cultural background and context.

Enjoying the Chinese abacus and you'll share the classic heritage of human civilization.

算盘是记录历史、传承文明的特殊载体。

中国算盘是我国古代劳动人民的伟大创造，它是在两千年前筹算的基础上演变而来的。据考证，中国算盘起源唐宋，盛行元明。中国算盘由框、梁、档和珠四部分组成。它最大的特质是有横梁；上一珠为五。中国算盘以其深邃的运算内涵被誉于世界上最古老、最简易的计算机。

本部分展示了60件中国算盘，汇聚了传统的实用中国算盘的精髓。按算珠的形状分有：圆形大型算盘、碟形中型算盘、菱形小型算盘、鼓珠算盘等；以构造分有：普通算盘、折叠算盘、无杆算盘、清盘算盘、定位算盘、显数算盘等；按材质分有：红木算盘、象牙算盘、汉白玉算盘、金质算盘、银质算盘、牛角算盘、翠翡算盘等。

中国算盘凝聚着我们祖先智慧与文明，承载着东方民族优秀文化的精粹，也反映了明清以来我国计算水平与成就。

欣赏这些中国算盘，让您深情触摸到中华传统文化底蕴与脉络。

品评这些中国算盘，与您分享人类文明遗产经典算盘的博大精深。

算盘起源系列——仿古算板
Origin abacus series—archaic abacus board

第一部分
Part I

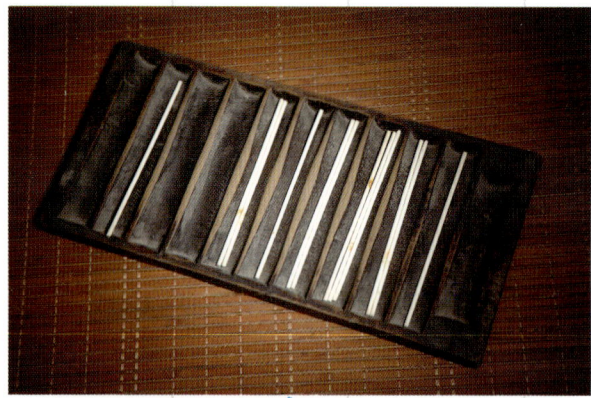

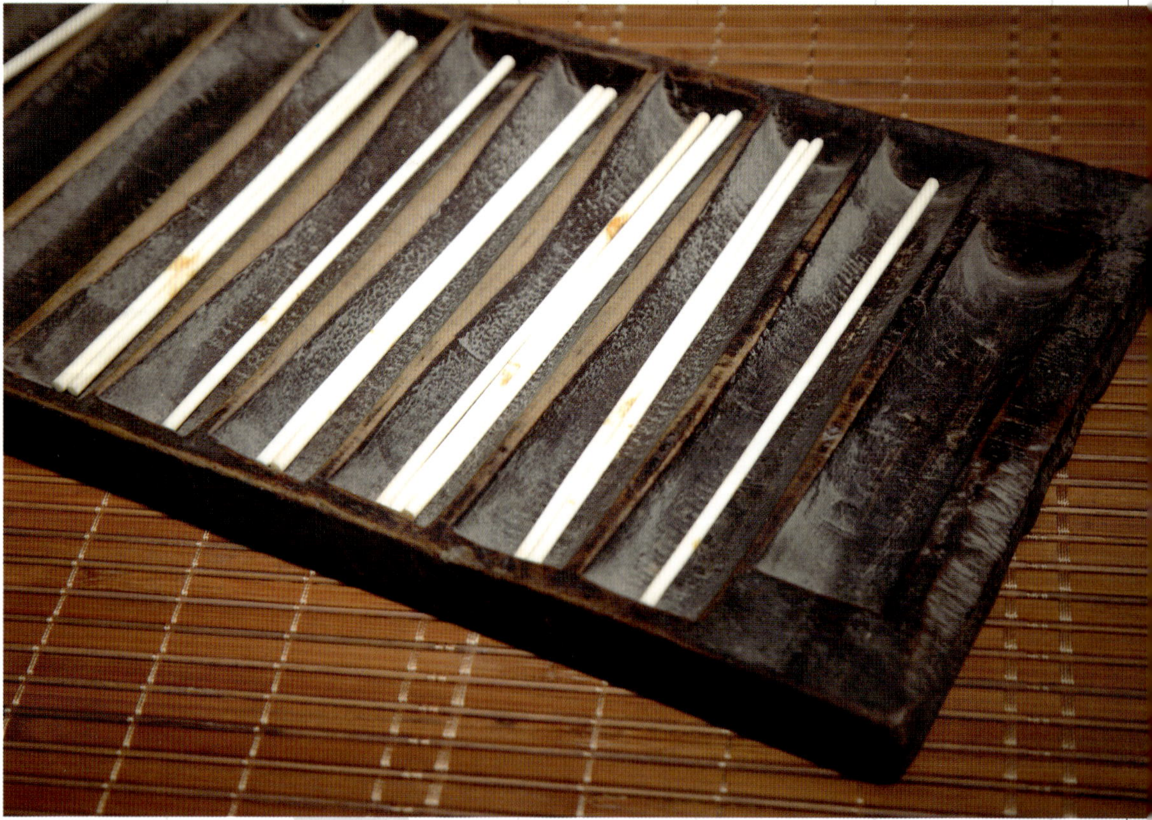

算盘起源系列——仿古算具、仿古陶丸及串档算珠
Origin abacus series—archaic calculating tods,
pottery beads and serial calculating beads

算盘起源系列——仿古算珠二颗
Origin abacus series—two archaic calculating beads

二五圆珠9档合式木质算盘（清代）
2—5 round beads，9 rods，well—formed wooden abacus（Qing Dynasty）

▲ 二五圆珠9档有底板象牙算盘（清代）
2—5 round beads, 9 rods, ivory abacus with seatboard(Qing Dynasty)

▲ 二五圆珠24档巨型太极木算盘（现代）
2-5 round beads, 24 rods,
giant eight-diagram-shaped
appetizer wooden abacus (modern times)

▲ 二五鼓珠11档合式陶瓷算盘（民国）
2—5 drum beads,11 rods,well—formed pottery abacus(Min Guo)

二五圆珠13档四边角垫式青玉石算盘 (民国)
2—5 round beads,13 rods cyan jade abacus with gaskets in the four corners(Min Guo)

二五圆珠160档4米长（可供多人使用）药房柜台木质算盘（现代）

2—5 round beads,160 rods,4 meters long,(for multiplayer)
long wooden abacus for drugstore's counter(modern times)

一四圆珠7档陶土算盘（清代）　　1—4 round beads, 7 rods, china clay abacus(Qing Dynasty)

二五鼓珠13档全象牙算盘（清代）
2-5 drum beads, 13 rods, entirely ivory abacus（Qing dynasty）

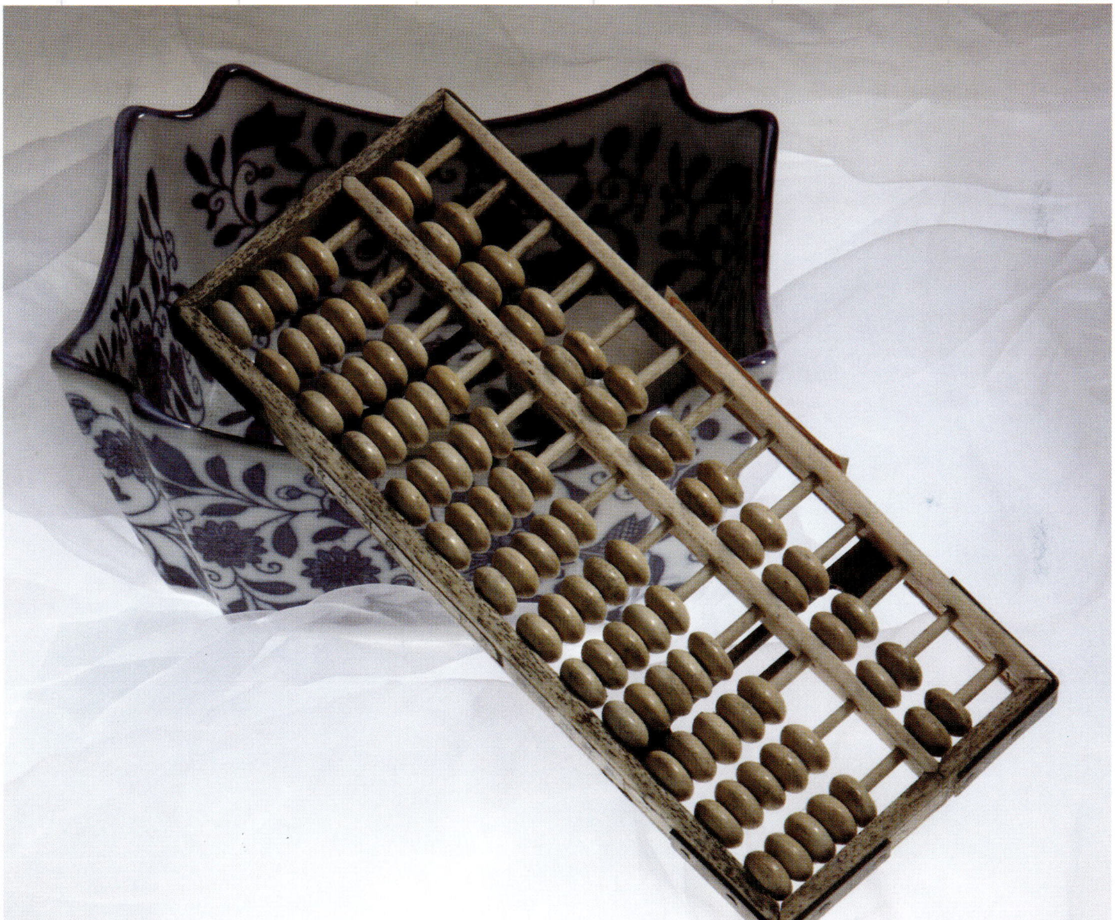

二五圆珠17档母子双亲白玉石算盘（民国）
2—5 round beads, 17 rods, diploid white jade abacus(Min Guo)

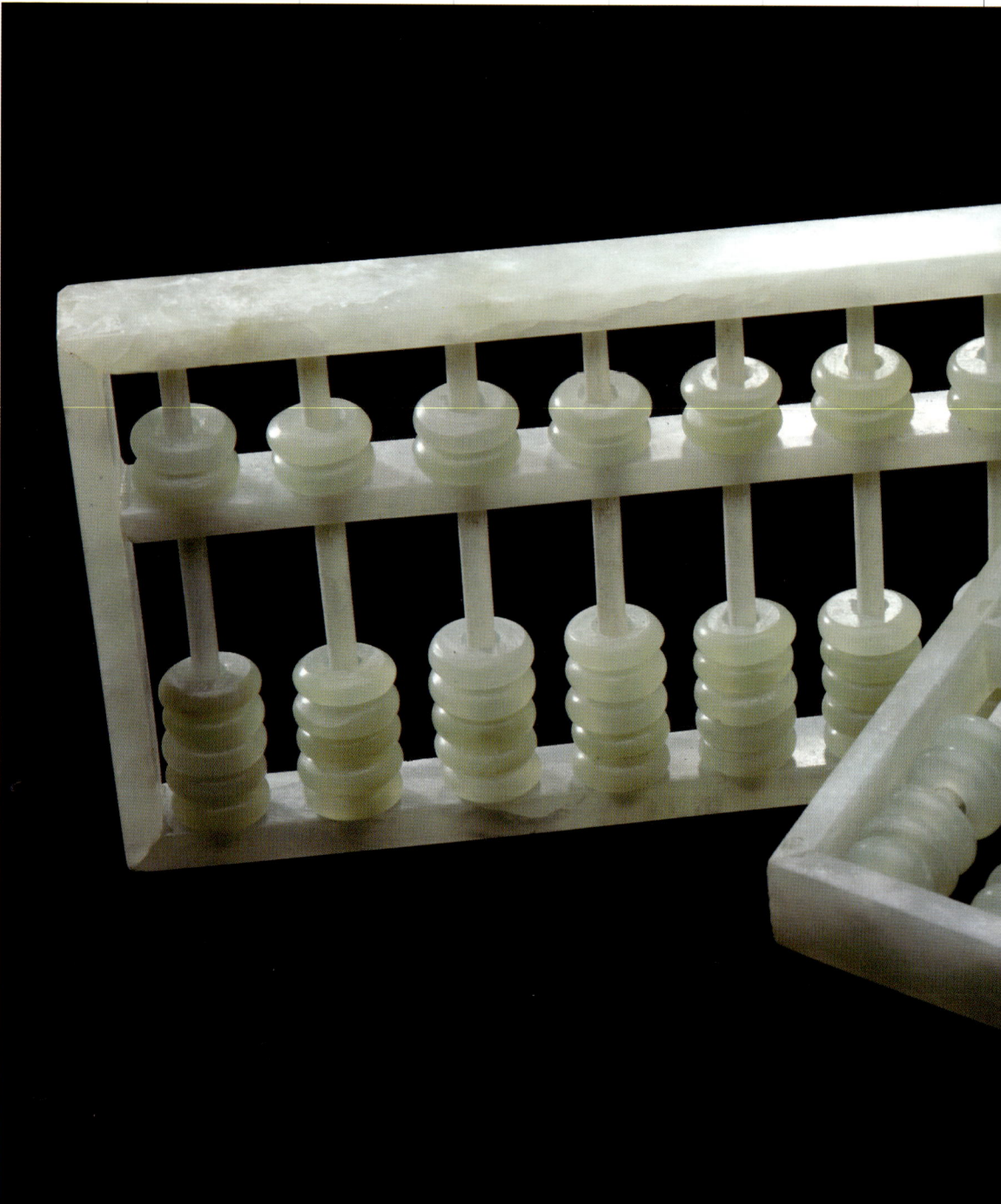

一四菱珠24档递进式圆形红木算盘（民国）
1—4 rhombus beads, 24 rods,
round rosewood step by step abacus (Min Guo)

三四圆珠13档双梁开方红木算盘（民国）
3-4 round beads, 13 rods, double beams,
rosewood abacus(Min Guo)

三五圆珠23档多功能红木算盘（现代）
3—5 round beads，23 rods，multi—use rosewood abacus（modern times）

二五圆珠11档双龙戏珠框边汉白玉算盘（民国）
2—5 round beads, 11 rods, white marble abacus
with two dragons playing with a pearl on the dack (Min Guo)

二五菱珠11档玻璃底板白玉算盘（民国）
2-5 rhombus beads,11 rods,white marble abacus with glass seatboard(Min Guo)

二五鼓珠13档有底板红木算盘（民国）
2—5 drum beads, 13 rods,
rosewood abacus with seatboard(Min Guo)

二五圆珠13档活底板红木算盘（清代）
2—5 round beads, 13 rods,
rosewood abacus with free seatboard(Qing Dynasty)

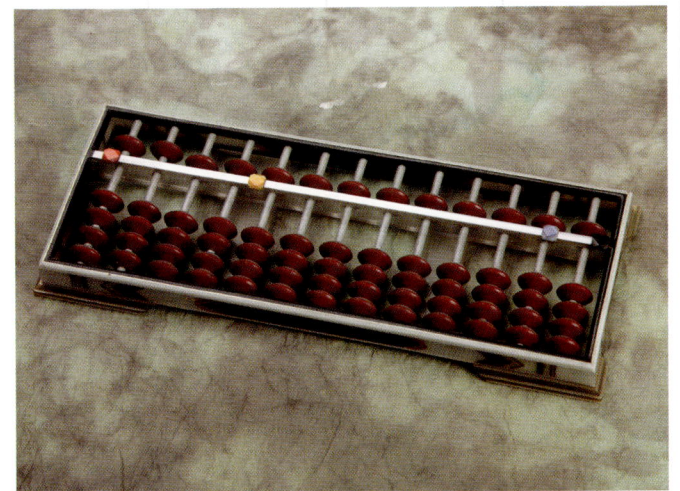

▲一四圆珠13档游标玉质算盘（现代）
1—4 round beads，13 rods，jade abacus with free tabs(modern times)

▲一四圆珠11档槽档全塑算盘（现代）
1—4 round beads, 11 rods, fully plastic abacus(modern times)

▲—四菱珠10档双梁正负数木质算盘（现代）
1—4 rhombus beads, 10 rods, double beam, positive negative number, wooden abacus(modern times)

中国实用算盘
Chinese Practical Abacus

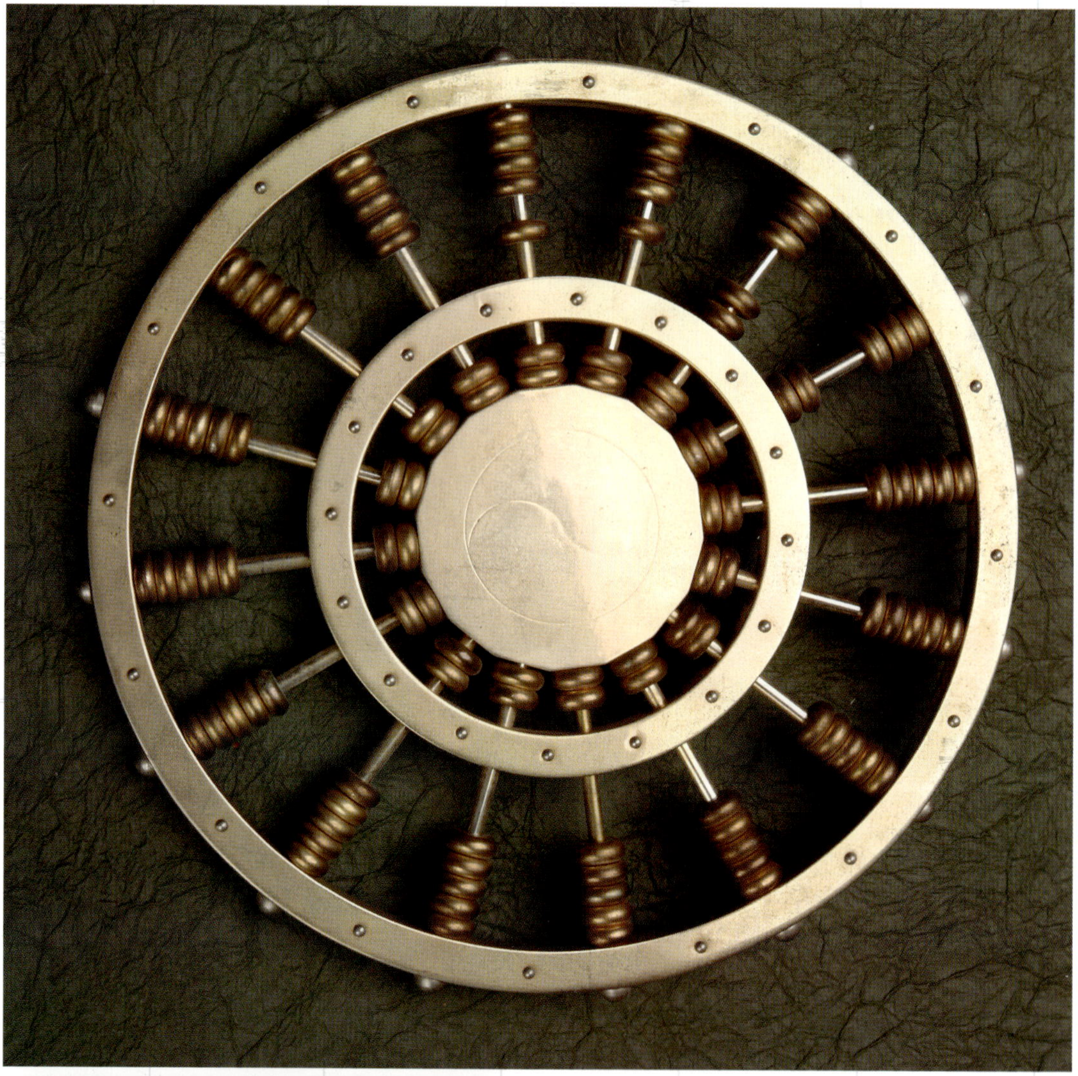

二五圆珠16档圆形铜质算盘（民国）
2-5 round beads, 16 rods,
round copper abacus(Min Guo)

▲一四菱珠13档龙凤框边象牙算盘（民国）
1-4 rhombus beads，13 rods，ivory abacus with Dragon and Phoenix on the deck(Min Guo)

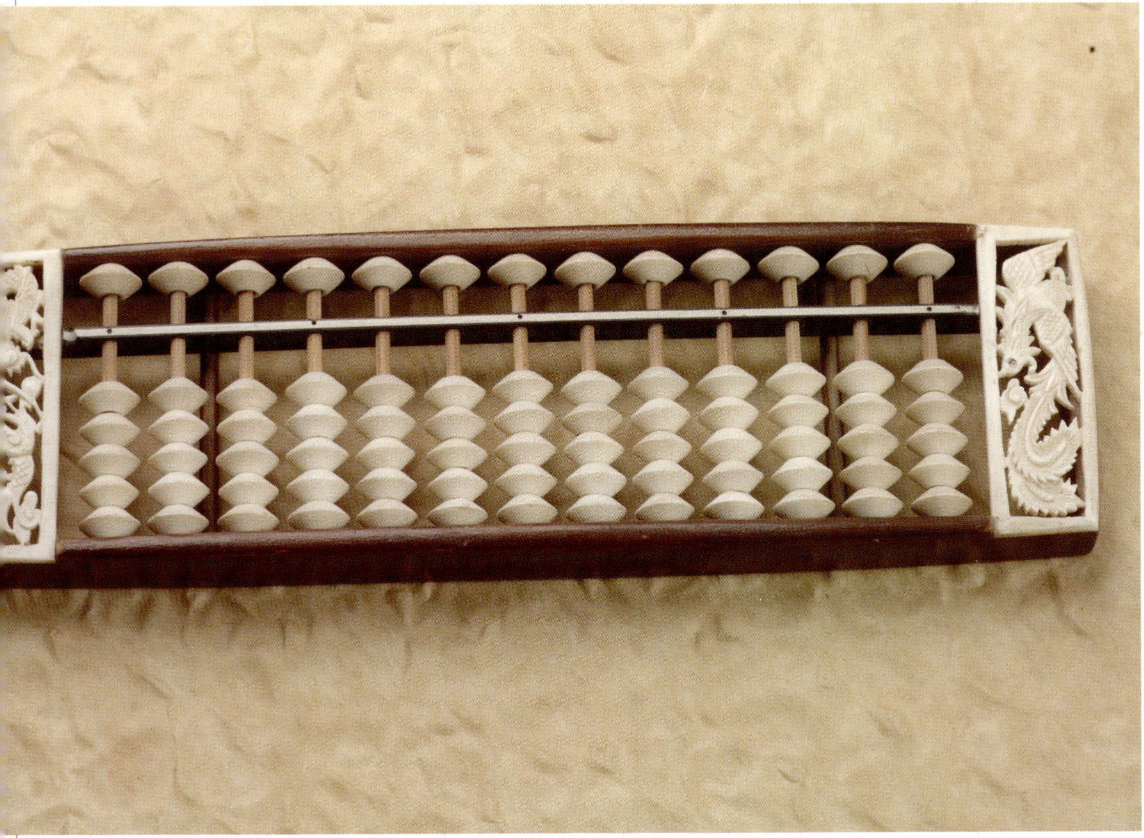

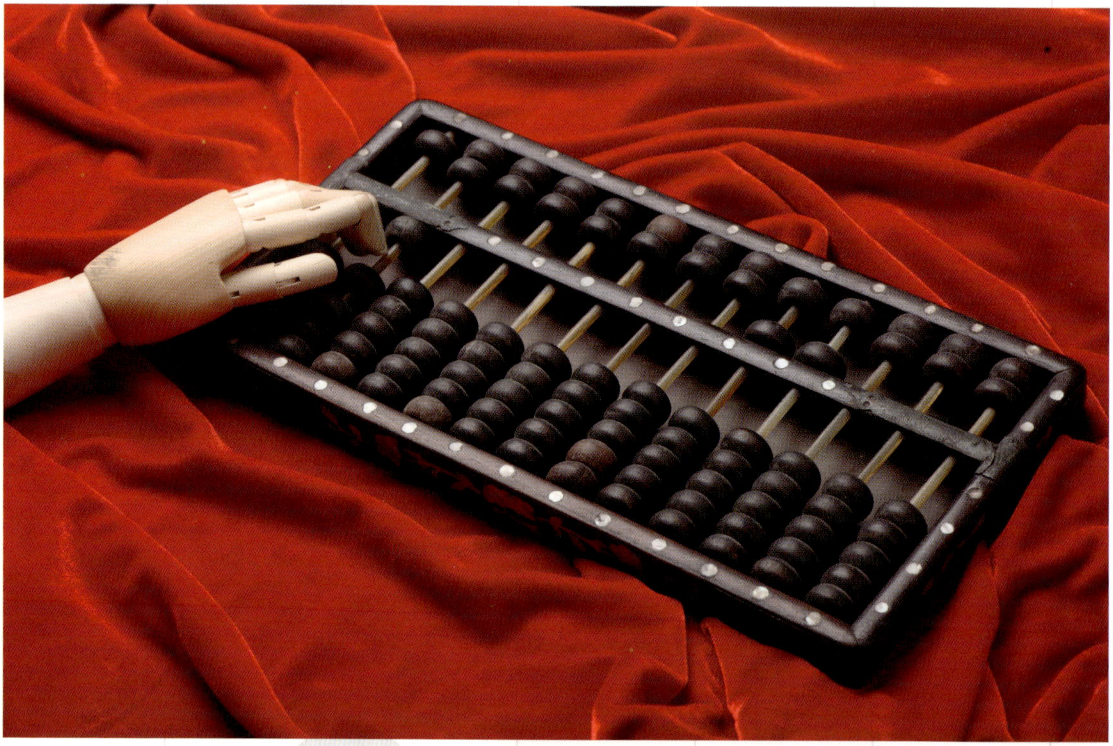

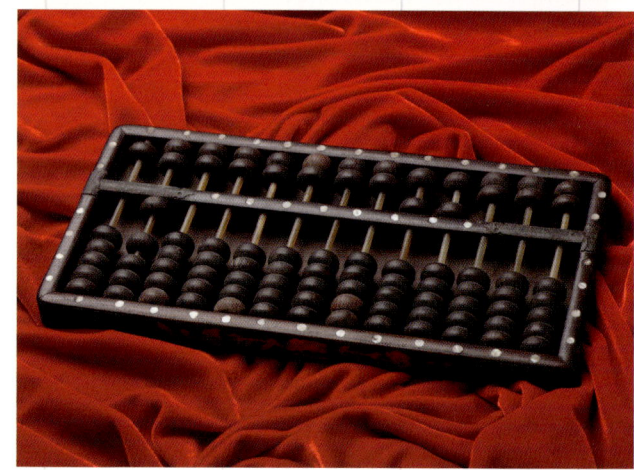

▲二五圆珠13档牛筋红木算盘（民国）
2—5 round beads，13 rods，ox tendon rosewood abacus（Min Guo）

红木算盘组合　　rosewood abacus series

▲二五菱珠10档棕毛教学木质算盘（民国）
2-5 rhombus beads,10 rods,palm fibre wooden teaching abacus(Min Guo)

二五鼓珠13档牛筋活底板红木算盘（清代）
2—5 drum beads，13 rods，ox tendon rosewood abacus with free seatboard(Qing Dynasty)

三五圆珠13档多功能(天三)木质算盘 (现代)
3—5 round beads, 13 rods, multi—use (3 on the top) wooden abacus (modern times)

一四圆珠13档标量红木算盘（民国）
1—4 round beads,13 rods,scalar quantity ,rosewood abacus(Min Guo)

二五圆珠23档有底板圆角框红木算盘（清代）
2—5 round beads, 23 rods, rosewood abacus with seatboard and round corner(Qing Dynasty)

二五鼓珠13档红木算盘（民国）
2—5 drum beads, 13 rods, rosewood abacus (Min Guo)

二五圆珠13档红木算盘（民国）
2—5 round beads，13 rods，rosewood abacus(Min Guo)

一五菱珠27档陶土算盘（民国）
1—5 rhombus beads, 27 rods,
pottery abacus(Min Guo)

一四菱珠17档学生学习木质算盘（现代）
1—4 rhombus beads, 17 rods, wooden abacus for the student(modern times)

一四圆珠12档折叠式象牙算盘（民国）　　1—4 round beads, 12 rods, folding ivory abacus (Min Guo)

仿古算盘合　archaic abacus

—四菱珠17档清盘木质算盘（现代）
1—4 rhombus beads, 17 rods, winding—up wooden abacus(modern times)

二五圆珠24档八卦太极有底板木质算盘（民国）
2—5 round beads, 24 rods,
eight—diagram—shaped appetizer wooden abacus
with seatboard(Min Guo)

一四菱珠13档合式木质算盘（现代）
1—4 rhombus beads，13 rods，well—formed wooden abacus（modern times）

二五圆珠13档黑玉石算盘（现代）　　2—5 round beads，13 rods，black jade abacus（modern times）

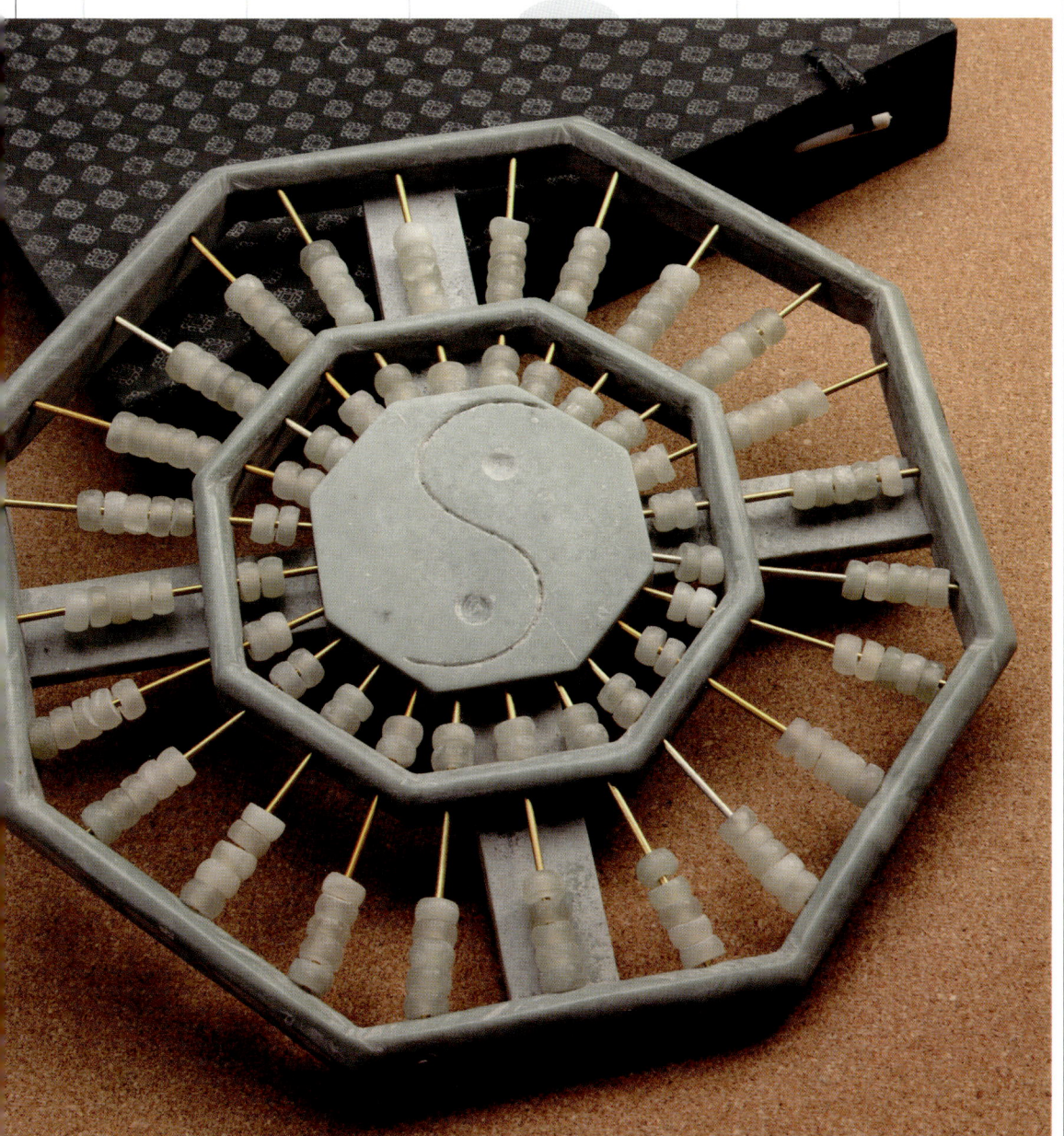

二五圆珠24档八卦大理石算盘（民国）
2—5 round beads,24 rods,eight—diagram—shaped appetizer marble abacus(Min Guo)

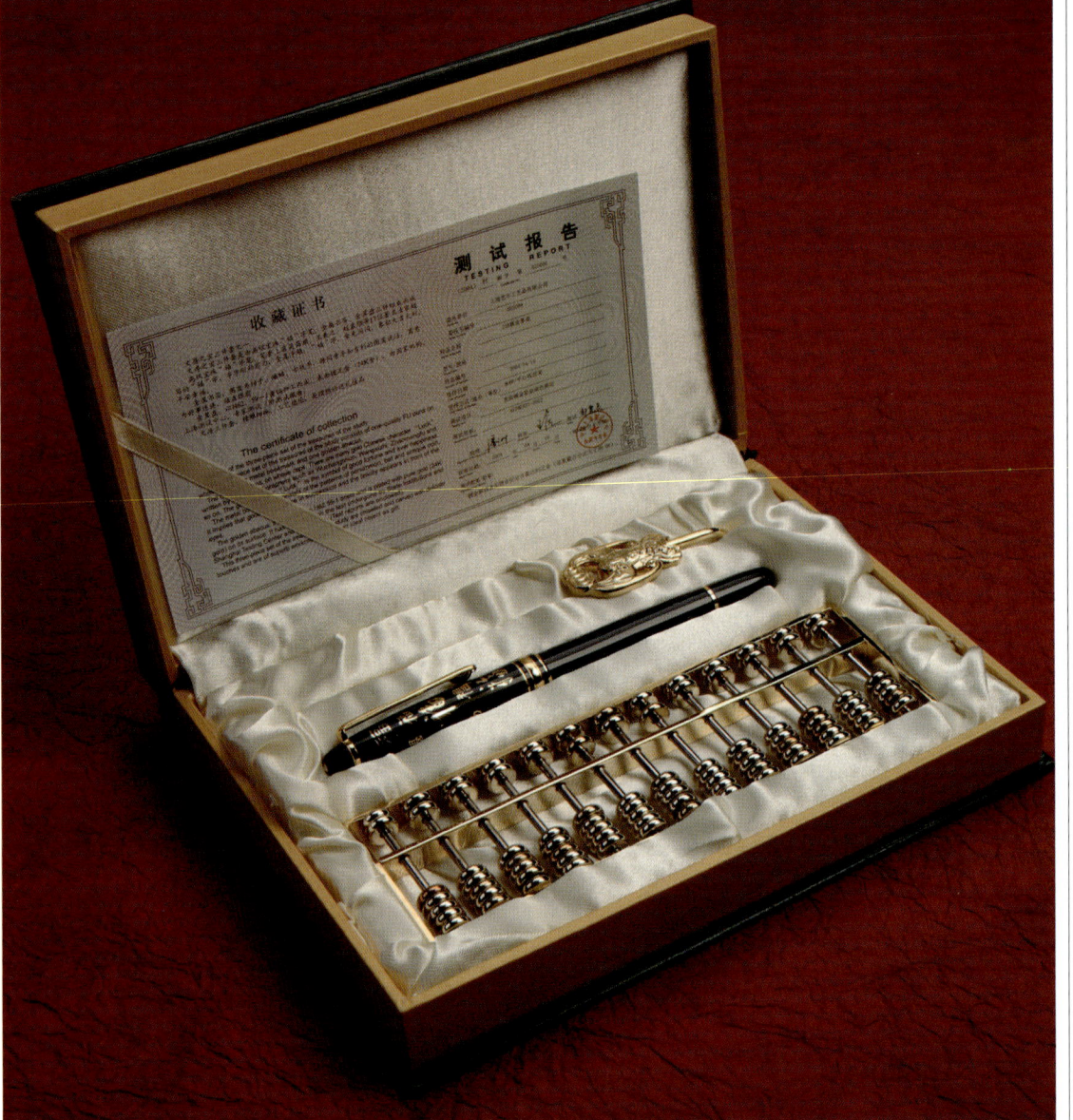

二五圆珠13档镀金算盘（现代）　　2—5 round beads, 13 rods, gold—plating abacus (modern times)

二五圆珠11档红木算盘（民国）　　2—5 round beads,11 rods,rosewood abacus(Min Guo)

二五鼓珠24档八卦太极大理石算盘（民国）
2—5 drum beads,24 rods,eight—diagram—shaped appetizer marble abacus(Min Guo)

二五圆珠18档如意图镀金算盘（现代）
2—5 round beads, 18 rods, gold—plating Ruyi graphic abacus(modern times)

盲人拨键变色全塑算盘（现代）
change colour when stirred,plastic abacus for the sightless(modern times)

一四半碟珠12档折叠式全塑算盘（现代）
1—4 half dish beads,12 rods,folding plastic abacus(modern times)

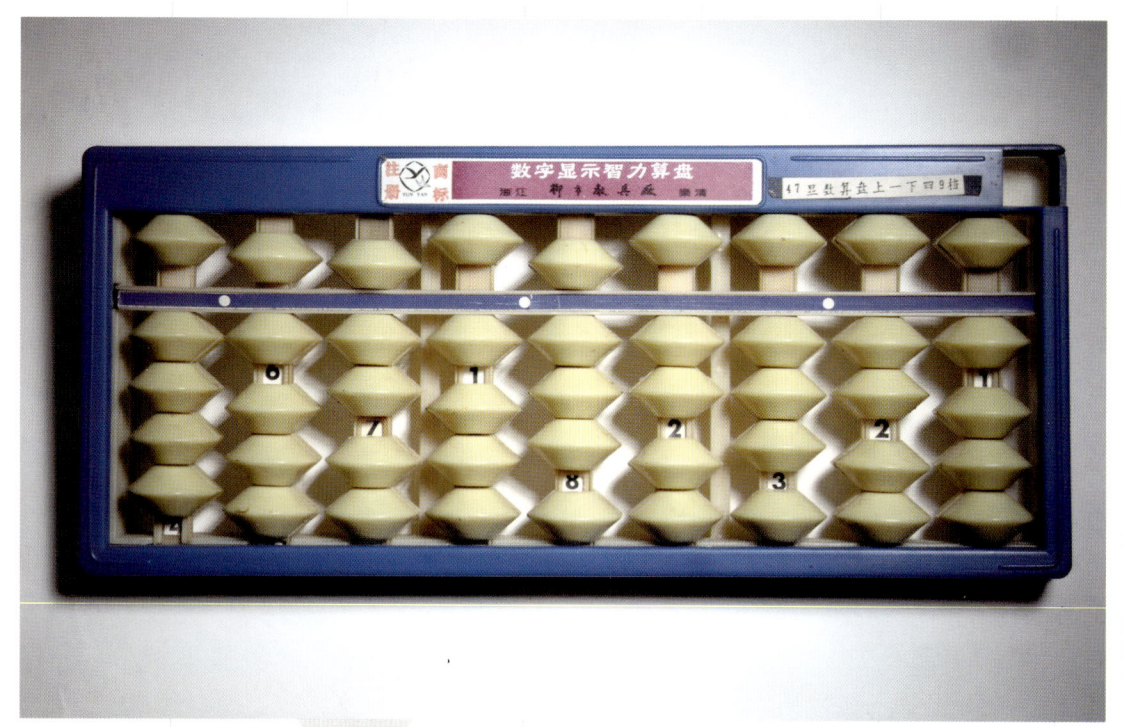

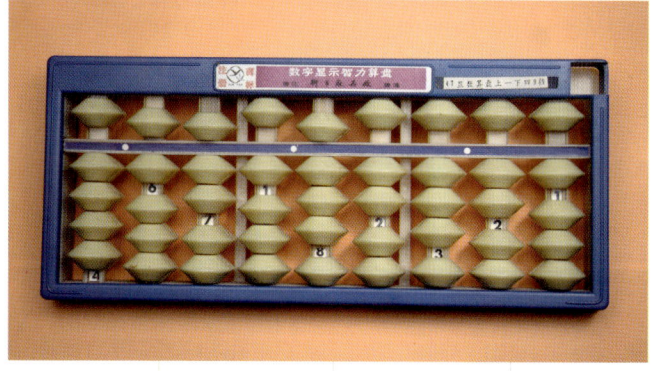

数字显示智力全塑算盘（现代）
number display intelligence fully plastic abacus(modern times)

一圆珠19档长条式木质算盘与二五圆珠11档红木算盘（现代）
1 round beads, 19 rods, long wooden abacus,
and 2—5 round beads, 11 rods, rosewood abacus(modern times)

55

二五圆珠11档多功能暗记式木质算盘（民国）
2—5 round beads, 11 rods, multi—use wooden abacus with secretmarks(Min Guo)

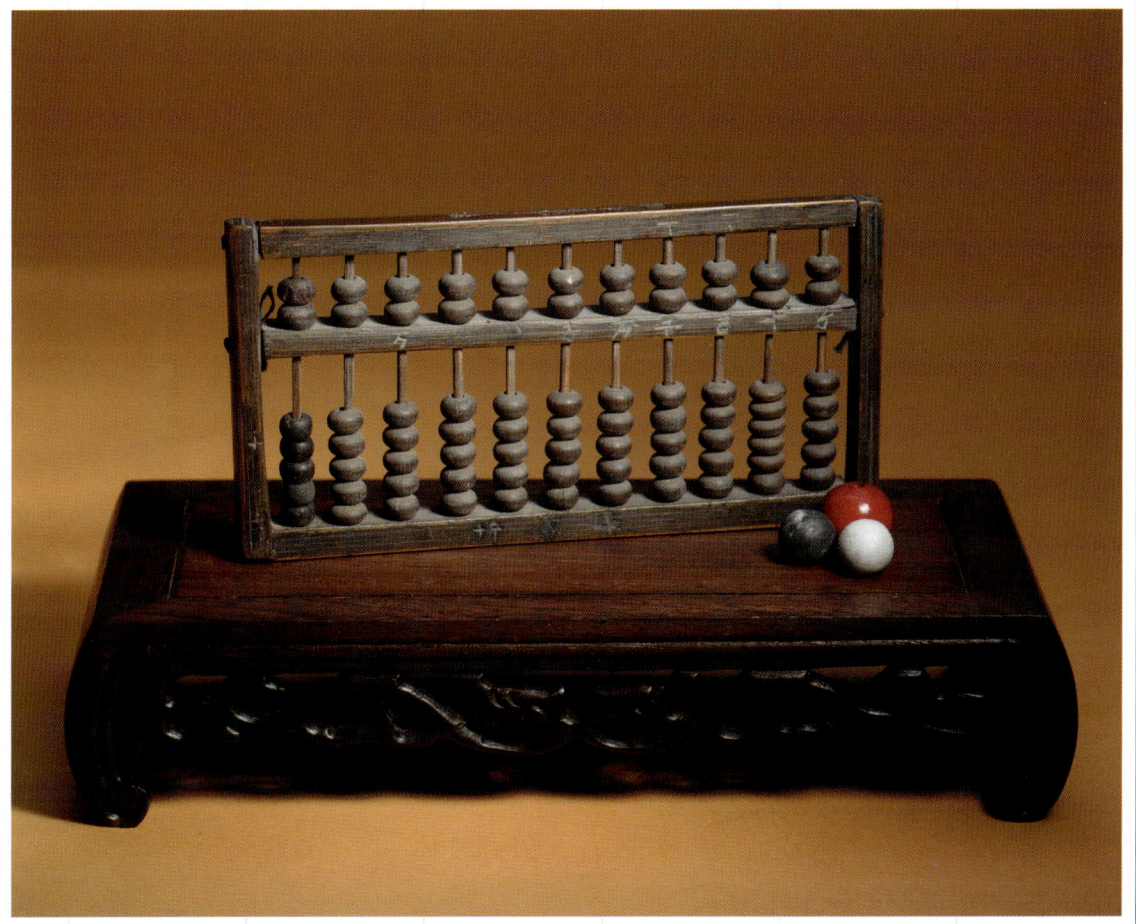

二五鼓珠11档竹质算盘（民国）　　2—5 drum beads , 11 rods , bamboo abacus (Min Guo)

四四圆珠13档木质算盘（民国）
4—4 round beads，13 rods，wooden abacus（Min Guo）

二五菱珠11档有底板合式木质算盘（民国）
2—5 rhombus beads,11 rods,well—formed wooden abacus with seatboard(Min Guo)

二五圆珠13档红木算盘（民国）
2-5 round beads, 13 rods,
rosewood abacus (Min Guo)

二五圆珠13档宫廷包金式木质算盘(民国)
2—5 round beads，13 rods，royal wooden abacus(Min Guo)

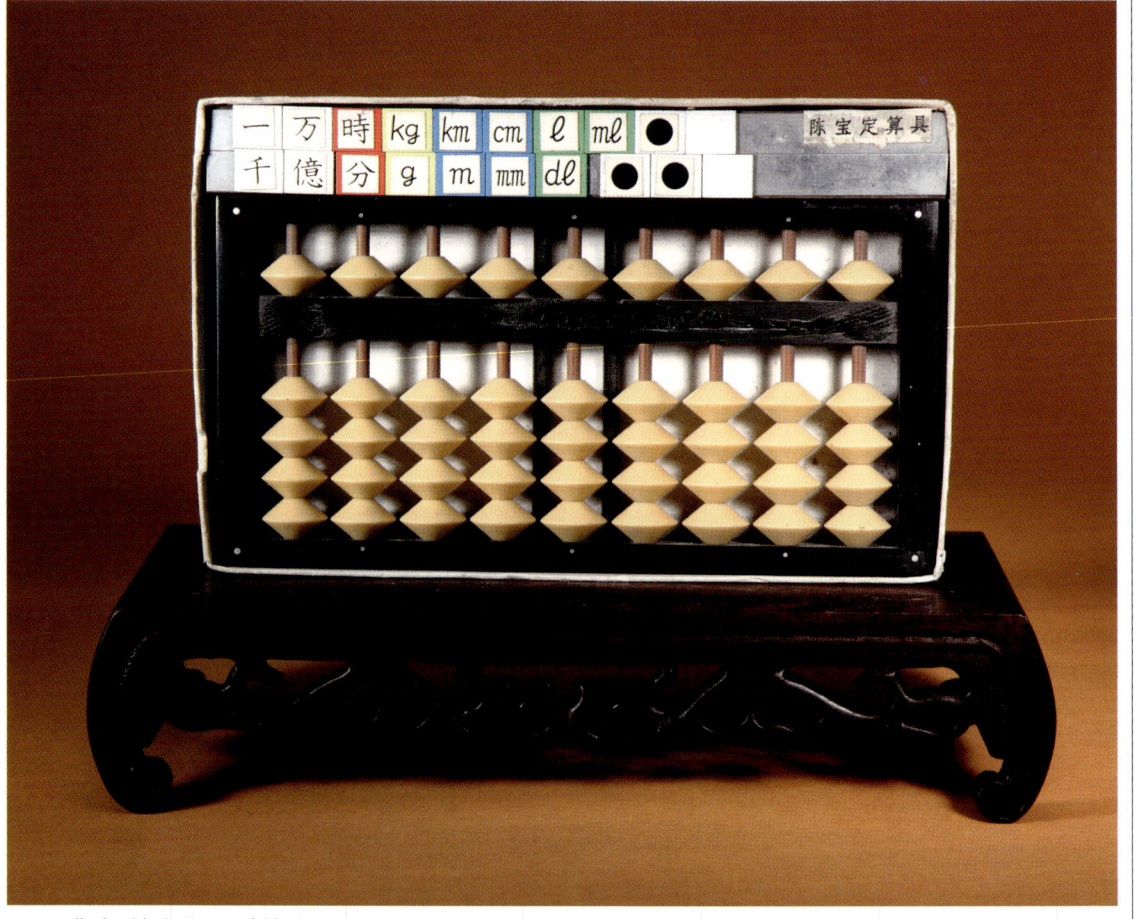

一四碟珠9档定位塑质算盘（现代）
1—4 dish beads，9 rods，plastic orientation abacus（modern times）

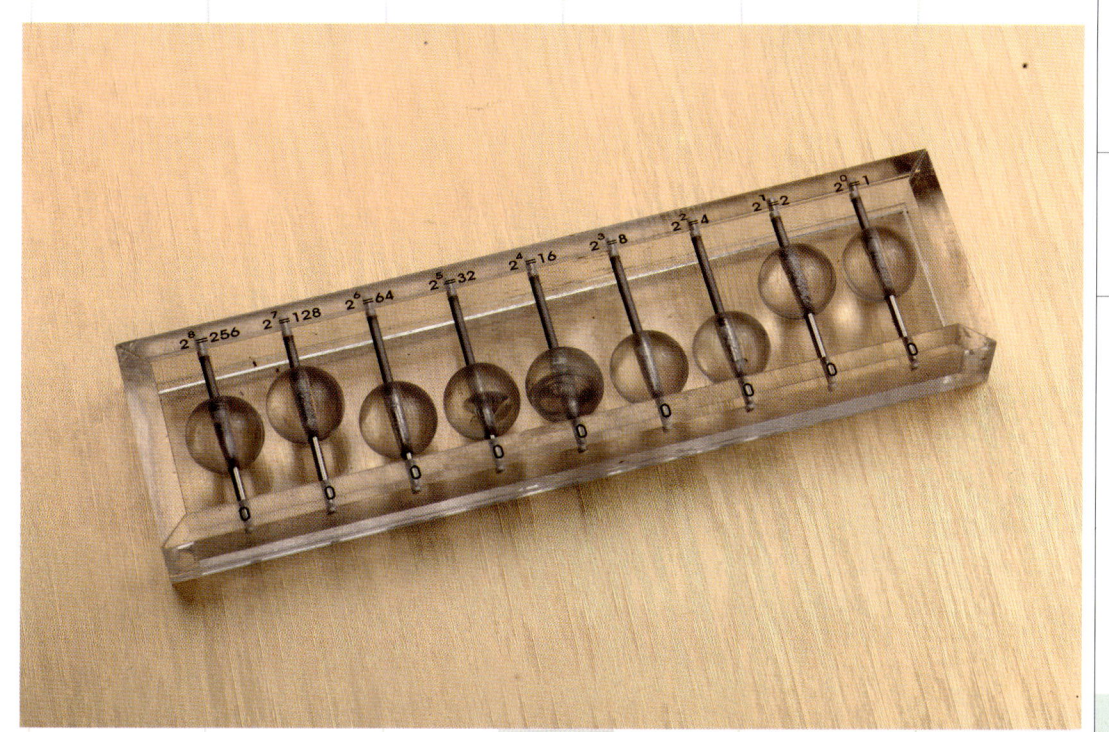

中国台湾·二进位算盘（现代）
Taiwan, China · binary bit abacus(modern times)

刻有 "善恶权由人自作，是非算定法难容"
对联的中国台湾二五鼓珠11档城隍庙祈福木质算盘（现代）
with antithetical couplat; "good and evil are performed by people,
right and wrong are judged by law"
Taiwan, China · 2—5 drum beads, 11 rods,
wooden blessing abacus from Chenghuang Temple (modern times)

In a sense, abacus is a symbol.

As the main computing tools, abacus is widely used in Qing Dynasty. It rooted deeply in civil society, and is given a whole new meaning ——"lucky" and "well-being". It became a fashion trend to furnish with abacus and sent abacus as a gift.

In particular, nowadays the craft abacus is branded the "send money" and "become rich" label, and becomes even more popular.

This section assembles 60 highly appreciated folk craft abaci. According to the purpose, there are: trimmings, decorations, daily appliances, display, gifts, etc.; according to the shape, there are: round, long, square, heart, cylinder, tower , etc.; according to the workmanship, there are: mosaic, ivory carving, miniature, painting, embroidery, Lou carving, etc.

Appreciating the folk craft abacus and you'll enjoy its simple spirit and internalized wisdom.

Enjoying the folk craft abacus and you'll feel its charm and sophisticated skills.

算盘在某种意义上是一个符号、一种象征。

清代盛世，算盘作为主流计算工具被广泛使用。在深入植根民间中，赋予了一个全新的寓意"招财"、"福祉"，这便成了文人雅士怡情养性的观赏陈设，也被庶民草根当作庆贺寿诞的馈赠礼品。以算盘为主题制作各式工艺品就成了一种时尚、一种格调，尤其是改革开放后商品经济高度发达的当下，工艺算盘打上了"发财"、"致富"的标签，尽显奢华富贵之风，备受世人的钟爱与推崇。

本部分荟集了60件有较高艺术欣赏价值又有实用意义的工艺算盘。按藏品用途分有：佩饰类、装饰类、日常器具类、陈设类、礼品类等；按造型形状分有：圆形、长形、方形、心形、筒形、塔形等；按工艺制作分有：镶嵌类、牙雕类、微雕类、绘画类、刺绣类、镂雕类等。

工艺算盘集"计算、文化、工艺"等元素为一体，是一群介于古代与现代之间的独特作品，完美诠释了历史上不同时期工艺特点与文化品位。

欣赏这些工艺算盘，让您领略算盘蕴含的质朴精神与内敛智慧。

品评这些工艺算盘，与您体验工艺算盘审美趣味与精良技艺。

▲—四圆珠8档手镯银质小算盘（清代）
1—4 round beads,8 rods,sliver bracelet abacus(Qing Dynasty)

镶嵌红玛瑙手镯铜质小算盘（民国）
agate bracelet with copper abacus(Min Guo)

二五圆珠9档双面·龙盘凤飞框微雕全象牙算盘（明代）
2—5 round beads，9 rods，
duoble sided minitype ivory abacus with Dragon and Phoenix on the deck(Ming Dynasty)

二五圆珠15档有底板白珍珠算盘（民国）
2—5 round beads, 15 rods, white pearl abacus with seatboard(Min Guo)

二五薄珠5档翡翠算盘（清代）
2-5 slim beads, 5 rods, jady abacus (Qing Dynasty)

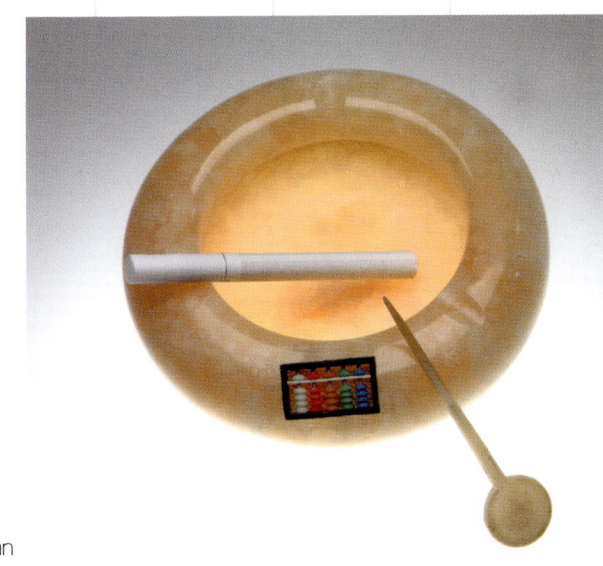

镶嵌烟灰缸彩色塑制小算盘（现代）
colourful plastic abacus within an
ashtray (modern times)

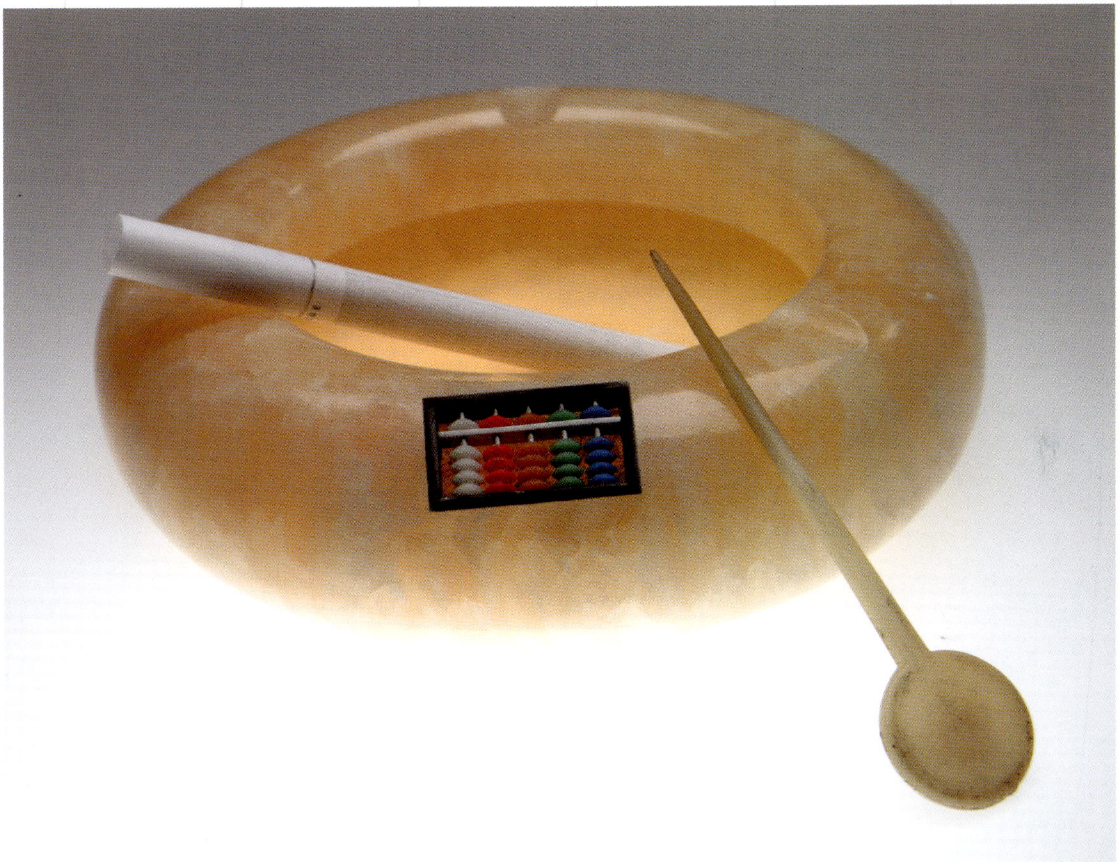

中国台湾·一四菱珠10档中华珠算学会纪念算盘（现代）
Taiwan，China·1—4 rhombus beads，10 rods，
souvenir abacus of Chinaese Abacus Association(modern times)

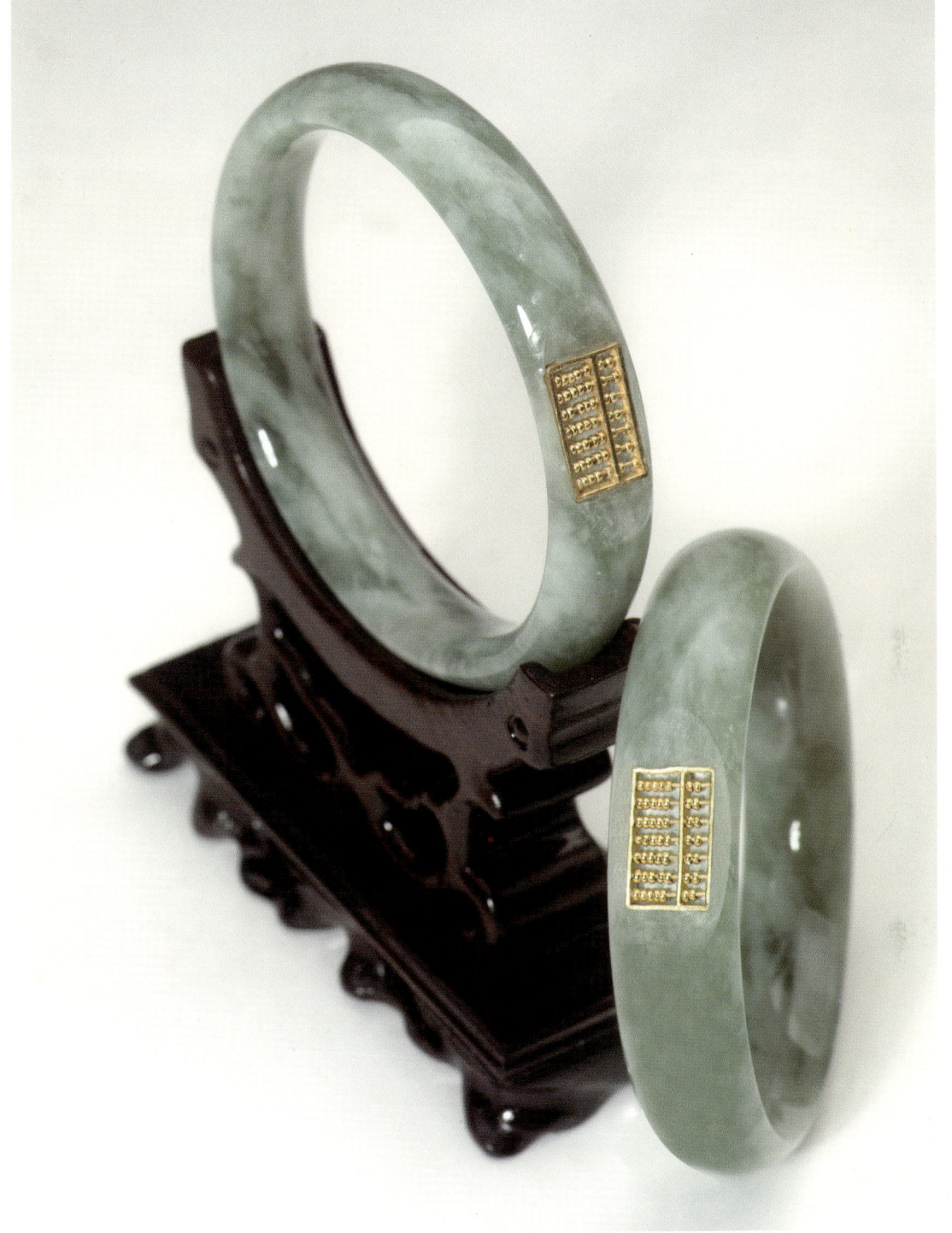

嵌金花珠玉镯算盘（民国）
jade bracelet with gold abacus(Min Guo)

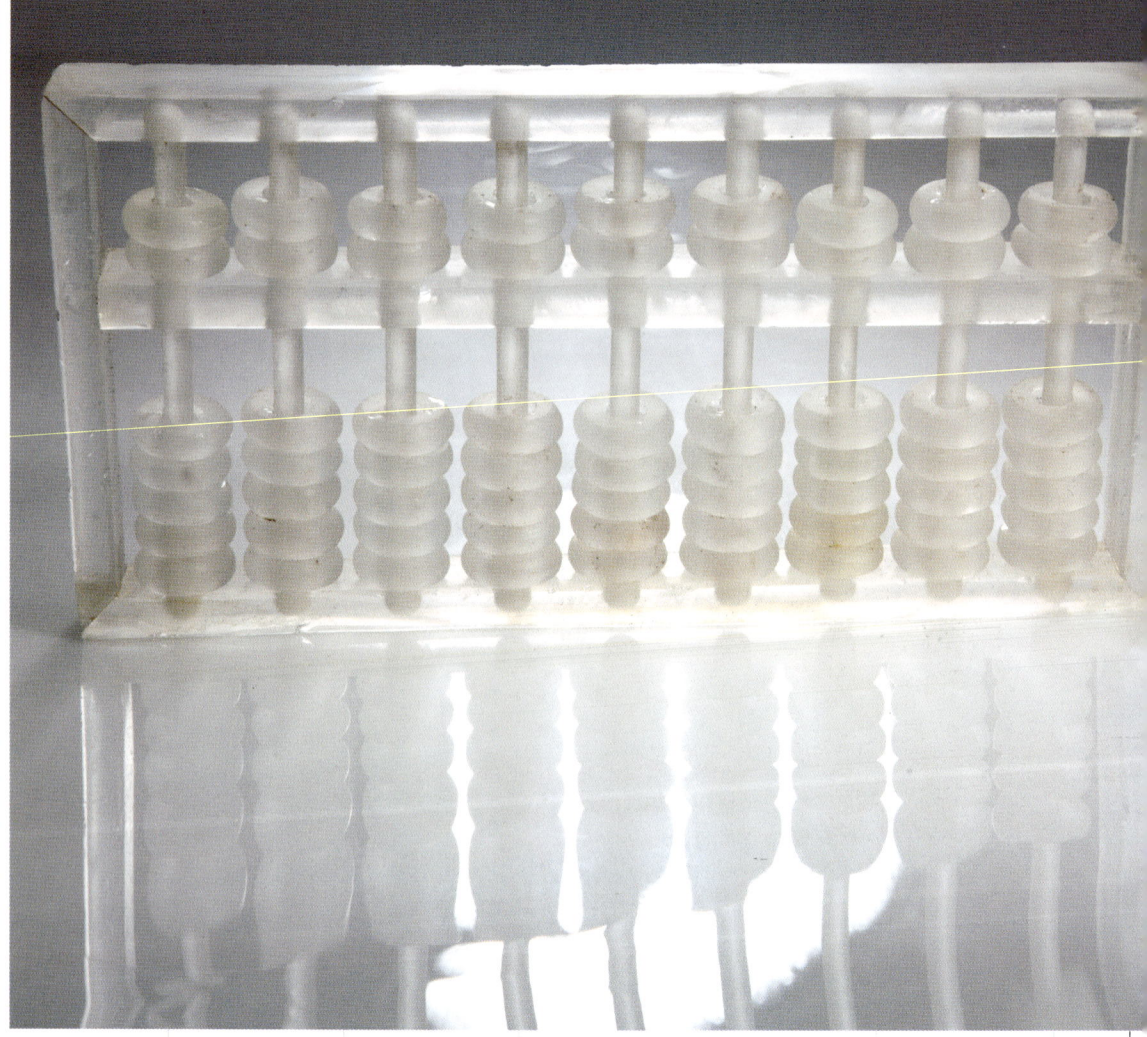

二五圆珠9档全水晶算盘（民国）
2—5 round beads, 9 rods, fully crystal abacus(Min Guo)

"不求人" 竹雕小算盘 (清代)
non—help bamboo abacus (Qing Dynasty)

二五圆珠11档如意铜质算盘（民国）　　2—5 round beads，11 rods，copper Ruyi abacus（Min Guo）

二五圆珠11档有底版全骨质算盘（民国）
2—5 round beads,11 rods, entirly bone abacus with seatboard(Min Guo)

▲—四菱珠13档笔筒式木质算盘（现代）
1—4 rhombus beads, 13 rods, column wooden abacus(modern times)

▲二五圆珠5档铜质手表算盘（现代）
2—5 round beads, 5 rods, copper watch abacus (modern times)

▲二五圆珠9档福寿钱夹银质算盘（清代）
2—5 round beads，9 rods，Fushou wallet silver abacus（Qing Dynasty）

▲旱烟杆吊饰金属小算盘（民国）
tobacco pipe with metal abacus（Min Guo）

▲二五圆珠8档发夹木质算盘（民国）
2—5 round beads, 8 rods, wooden hairpin abacus(Min Guo)

首饰算盘（现代）
jewelry abacus(modern times)

▲二五圆珠9档 "佛字" 银饰物银质小算盘（民国）
2—5 round beads, 9 rods, small sliver abacus with character in it(Min Guo)

▲二五圆珠7档银戒指银质小算盘（清代）
2—5 round beads, 7 rods, small sliver ring abacus(Qing Dynasty)

▲二五圆珠8档红玛瑙戒指铜质小算盘（民国）
2—5 round beads,8 rods, agate ring with copper abacus(Min Guo)

▲镌刻红玉心形吊饰金属小算盘（民国）
small metal abacus in heart—shaped ruby pendant(Min Guo)

▲一四圆珠2档纯金框白珠吊饰小算盘（清代）
1—4 round beads, 2 rods, gold deck abacus with white beads and pendant(Qing Dynasty)

饰品算盘系列
pendant abacus series

民俗工艺算盘
Folk Craft Abacus

一四圆珠11档白珍珠算盘（近代）
1—4 round beads, 11 rods, white pearl abacus(modern times)

▲—四菱珠1—30档塔形立体木质算盘（现代）
1—4 rhombus beads, 1—30 rods,
turriform solid wooden abacus(modern times)

第二部分
Part Ⅱ

苏绣算盘（现代）
Suzhou embroidery abacus(modern times)

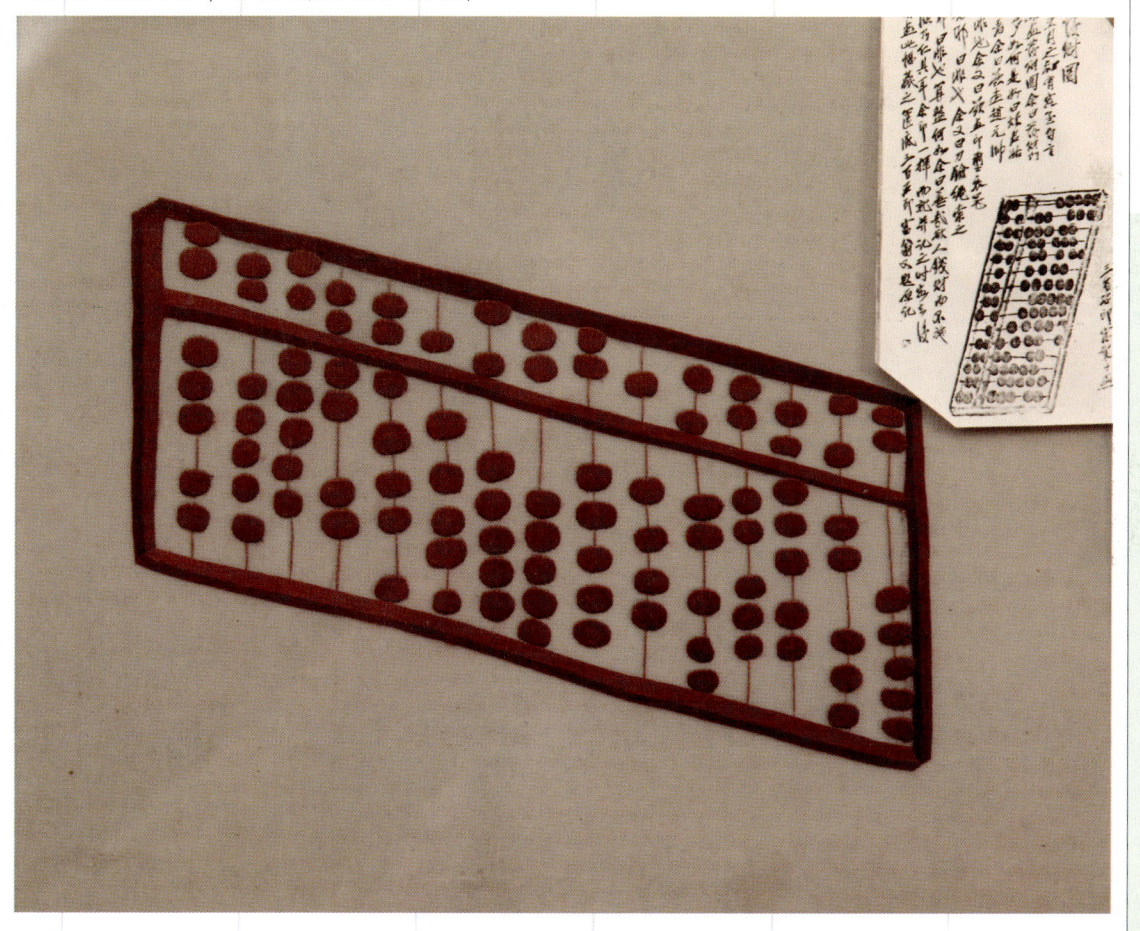

剪纸算盘（现代）
paper—cut abacus(modern times)

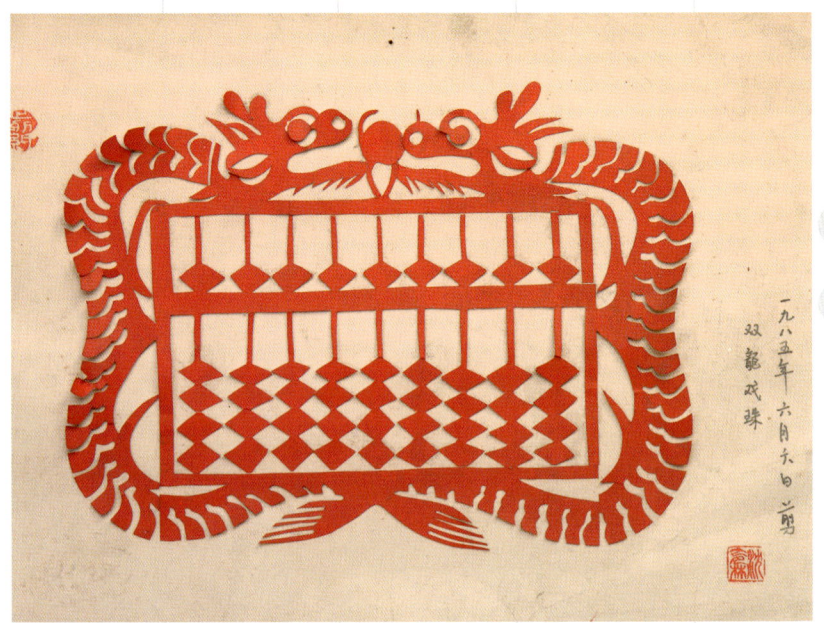

二五圆珠5档平面式奇石小算盘（现代）
2—5 round beads,5 rods,complanate bizarre stone abacus(modern times)

二五莲花珠9档象牙算盘（民国）
2—5 lotus beads, 9 rods, ivory abacus(Min Guo)

"账房先生与算盘" 立体铜质像（民国）
solid "accountant and abacus" bronze statue(Min Guo)

一四圆珠5档红玛瑙算盘（清代）
1—4 round beads, 5 rods, agant abacus(Qing Dynasty)

二五圆珠9档红玉算盘（民国）　2—5 round beads, 9 rods, ruby abacus(Min Guo)

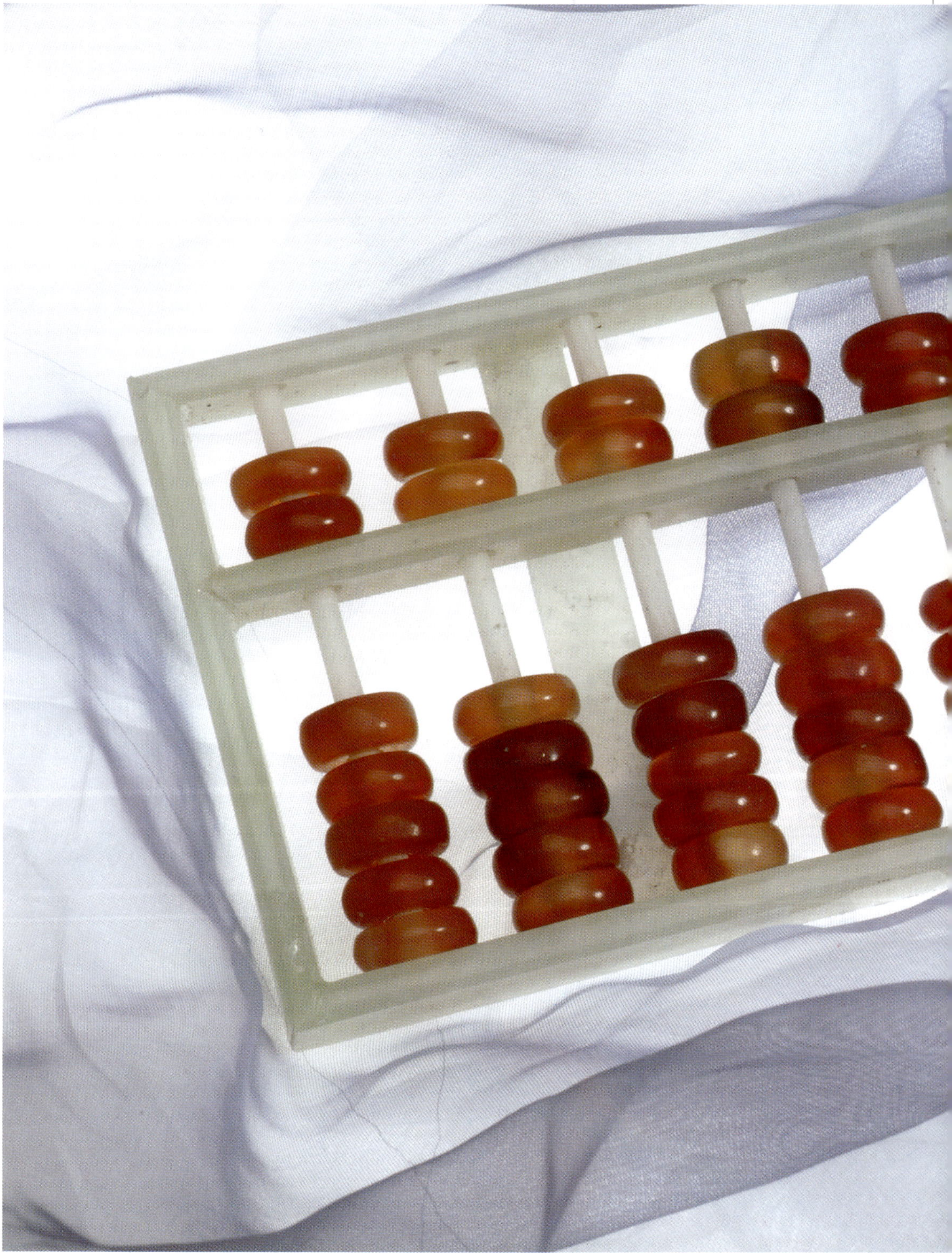

民俗工艺算盘
Folk Craft Abacus

二五圆珠13档红玉算盘（民国）
2—5 round beads,13 rods,ruby abacus(Min Guo)

一四圆珠10档景泰蓝算盘（民国）
1—4 round beads, 10 rods, cloisonne abacus(Min Guo)

第二部分
Part Ⅱ

一五菱珠15档座式屏风木质算盘（民国）
1—5 rhombus beads, 15 rods, wooden abacus screen(Min Guo)

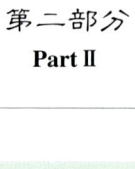

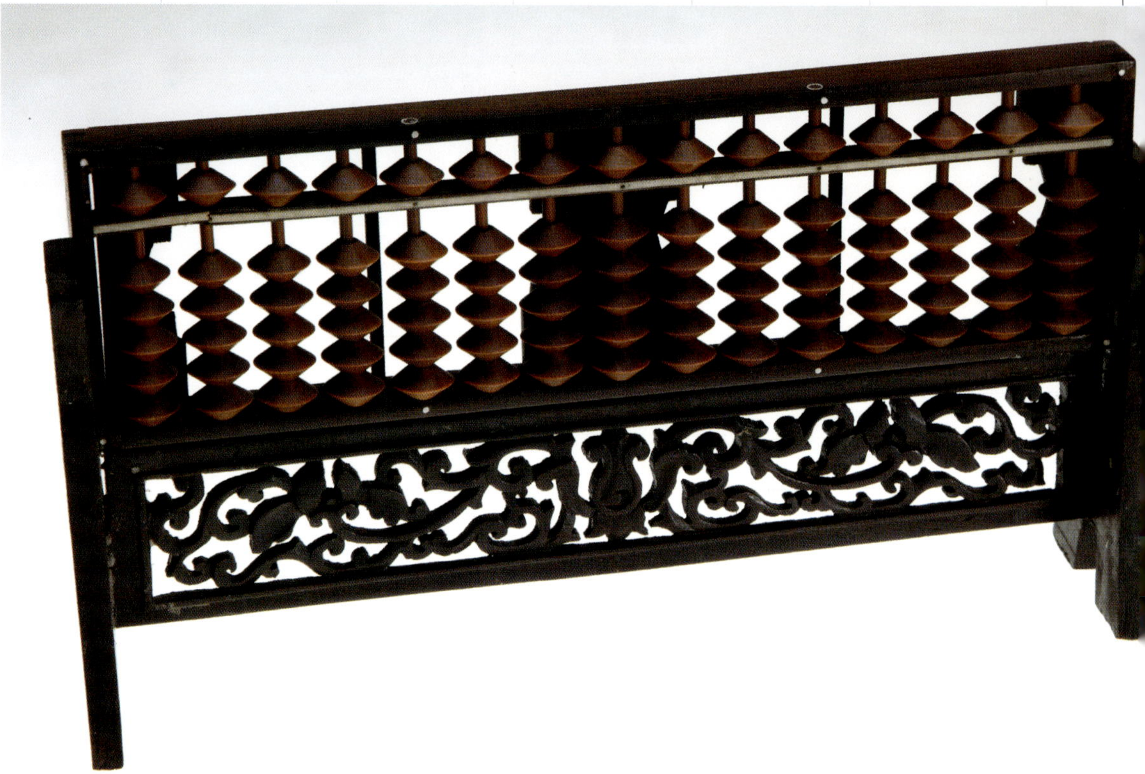

二五菱珠10档礼品青玉石算盘（民国）
2—5 rhombus beads, 10 rods, cyan jade abacus gift(Min Guo)

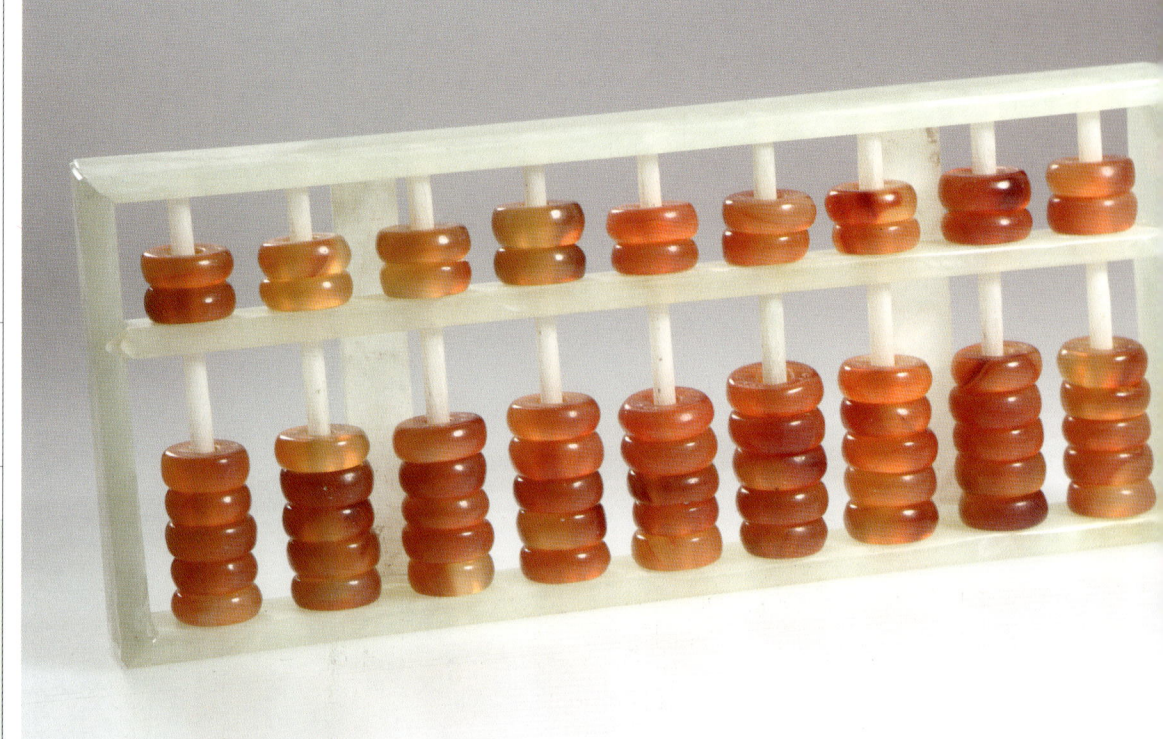

二五圆珠9档红玉算盘（民国）
2—5 round beads, 9 rods, ruby abacus(Min Guo)

二五圆珠9档挂式红木小算盘（清代）
2—5 round beams, 9 rods,
small hanging rosewood abacus（Qing Dynasty）

印有"齐白石发财图"算盘的真丝手绢（现代）
silk handkerchief with Fa Cai Tu drawn by Qi Baishi(modern times)

嵌刻旱烟壶盖上金属小算盘（民国）
small metal abacus on tobacco pot（Min Guo）

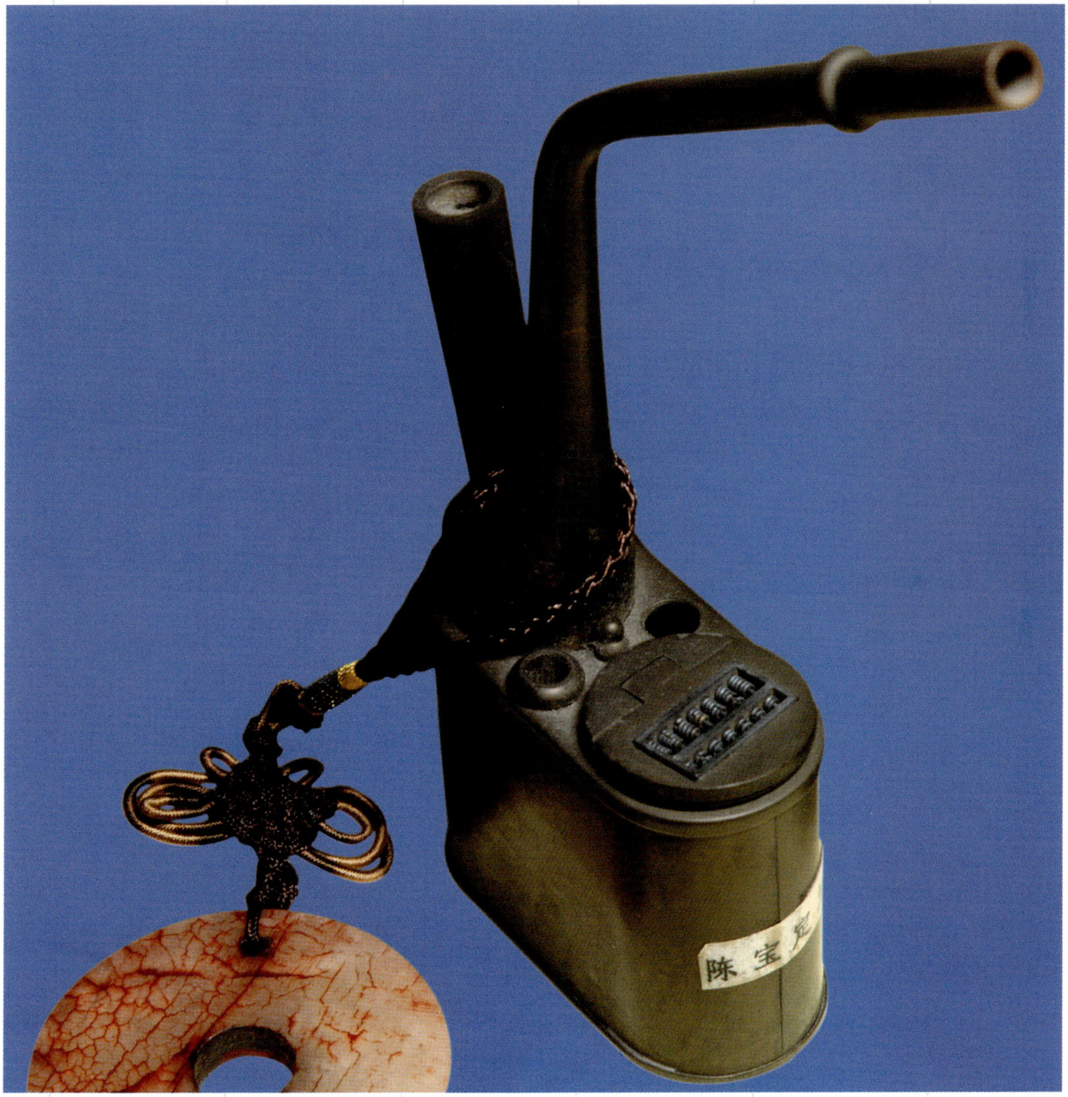

中国香港·二五圆珠8档祈福镀金算盘（现代）
Hong Kong, China·2—5 round beads, 8 rods, gold—plating blessing abacus(modern times)

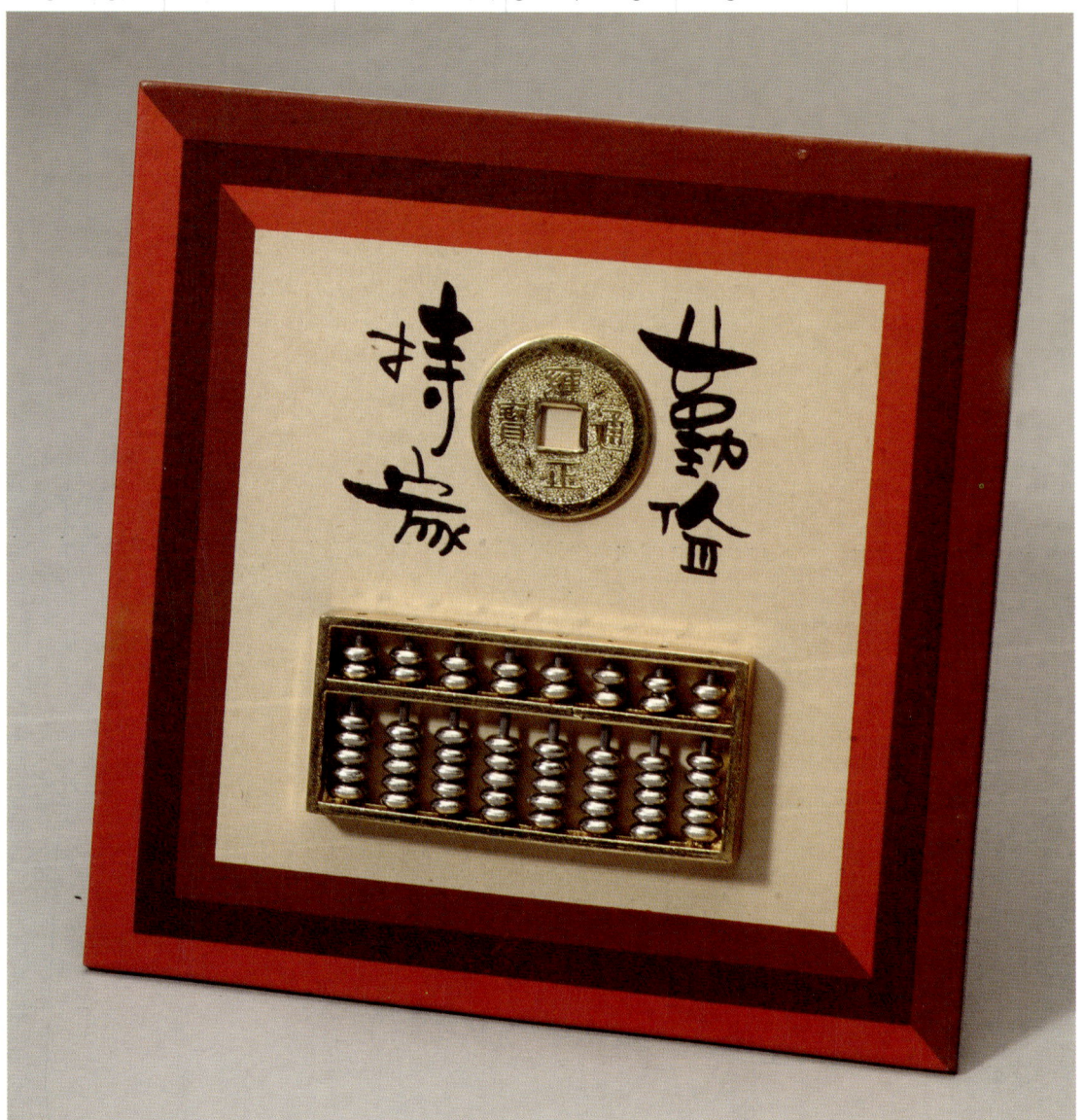

中国澳门·二五鼓珠9档钥匙吊饰不锈钢算盘（现代）
Macao，China·2—5 drum beads，9 rods，stainless steel abacus as a key pendant（modern times）

一四圆珠2档纯银框翠玉吊饰小算盘（民国）
1—4 round beads, 2 rods, small sliver deck abacus as a pendant (Min Guo)

纯金戒指算盘（民国）
gold ring abacus(Min Guo)

▲二五圆珠9档双面微雕象牙算盘（明代）
2—5 round beads, 9 rods, double—side miniature carved ivory abacus(Ming Dynasty)

▲二五圆珠5档超微雕象牙算盘（用细纱悬吊）（现代）
2—5 round beads,5 rods,super miniature carved ivory abacus(hung by slim string)(modern times)

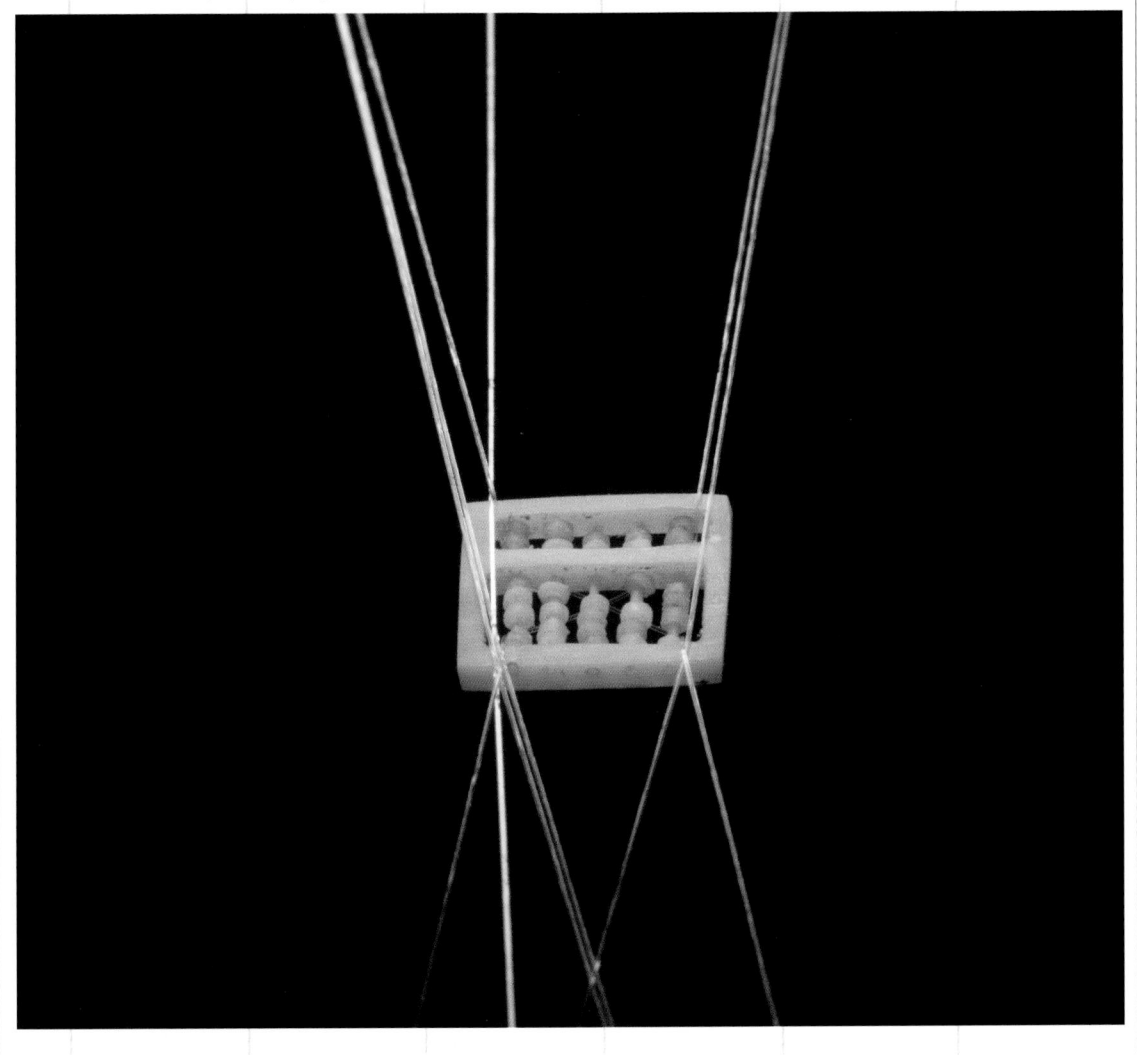

二五游珠9档针拨铜质算盘（清代）
2—5 rove beads, 9 rods, stir by needle, sliver abacus (Qing Dynasty)

二五圆珠11档双面挂式微雕象牙算盘（明代）
2—5 round beads,11 rods,
hangable double sided mintype
ivory abacus(Ming Dynasty)

嵌银质小算盘百年筛吉祥物挂件（清代、民国）
small silver abacus as a mascot(Qing Dynasty, Min Guo)

嵌银质算盘"庆生"百年筛吉祥物挂件（清代）
sliver mascot pendant（Qing Dynasty）

一四菱珠11档彩色珍珠项链算盘（现代）
1—4 rhombus beads,11 rods,colourful pearl necklace abacus (modern times)

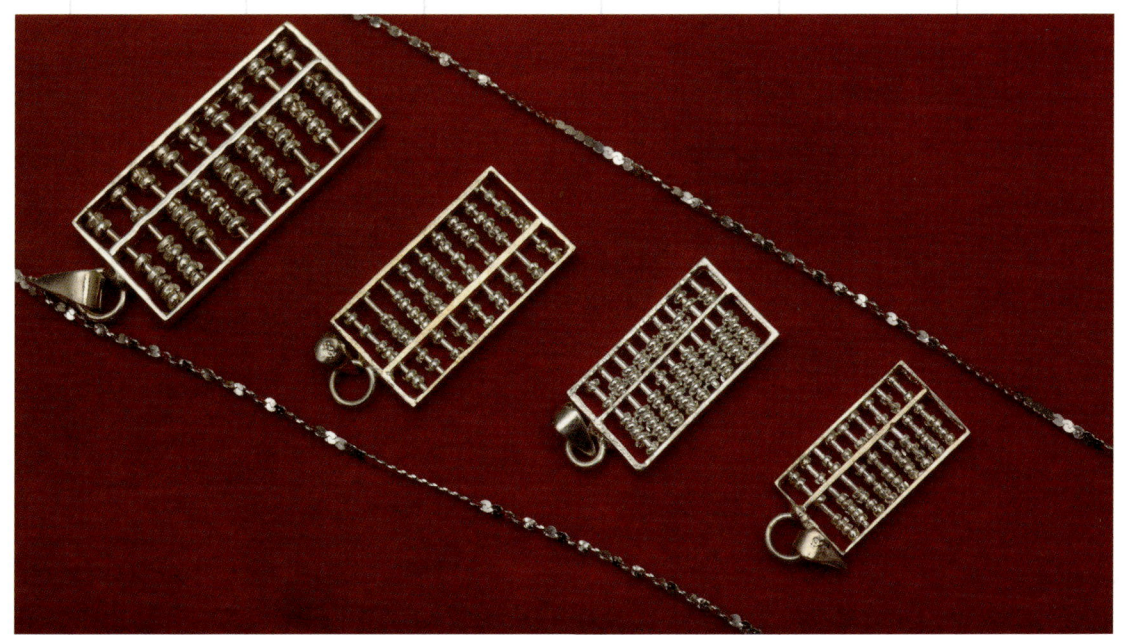

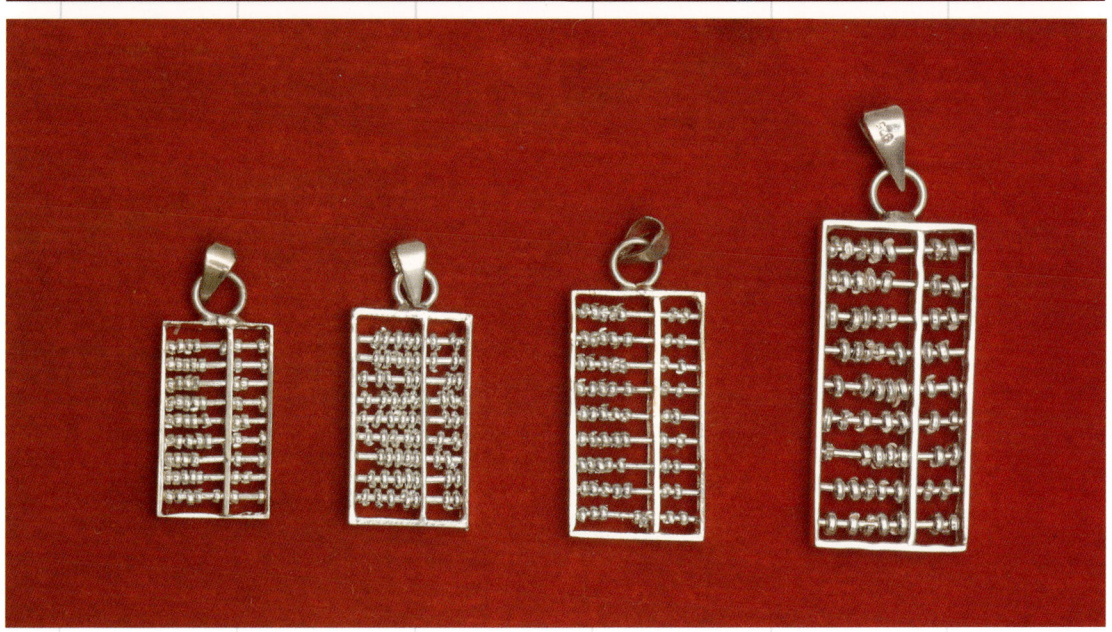

银质吊饰算盘系列（民国）
sliver abacus pendant（Min Guo）

白银耳环算盘（民国）
sliver ring abacus(Min Guo)

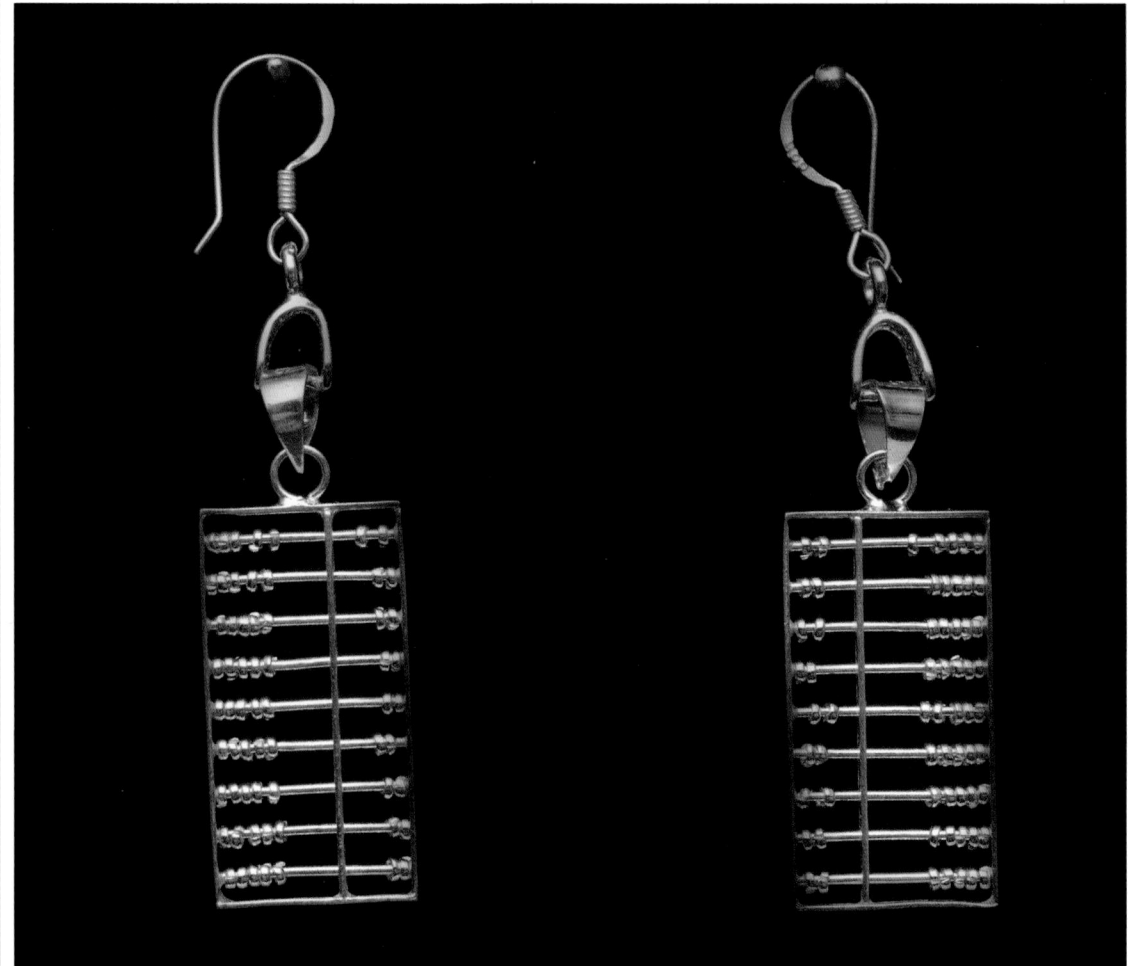

金项链算盘及吊饰系列（清代、民国）
gold necklace abacus and pendant series(Qing Dynasty, Min Guo)

民俗工艺算盘
Folk Craft Abacus

"恭喜发财"、"一路发"算盘挂件（现代）　　wish prosperity abacus pendant（modern times）

Abacus is an important contribution of China to the world culture.

Five hundred years ago (Ming Dynasty), Chinese abacus was introduced to Japan and Korea, and then to southeast Asian countries, Europe and America, where it rooted, bloomed and bron fruits. This brings very huge influence on world culture, society and economy. At the same time, based on the absorption of the wisdom of Chinese abacus, and grafting it with their own culture, these countries developed unique abacus culture.

This section shows more than 30 foreign abaci from different countries. According to the countries, there are: Japan, U.S., Russia, India, Malaysia and Korea, etc.; according to the functions there are: practical, teaching, art, festive and professional, etc.

These 30 abaci are not only a quintessence of the fusion of Chinese culture and foreign cultures, but also a platform to show foreign economy, science and technology, culture creativity and humanities manners. They are also a direct witness of Chinese Culture's openness.

Appreciating the foreign abacus and you'll realize the stature of human culture's built together, share together and win together.

Enjoying the foreign abacus and you'll know the long history of Chinese and foreign abacus culture exchange.

算盘是中华民族对世界文明的一项重要贡献。

500年前（明代），中国算盘先传入日本、朝鲜，后传到东南亚诸国、欧洲大陆、美洲各地，在那里生根、开花、结果，对世界文化、社会、经济带来了巨大影响。同时，世界各国在吸纳、借鉴中国算盘中精华，融会、坚持本土化基础上，开创了独具特色的算盘文化。

本部分展现了一些国家颇有代表性的算盘。按国度分有：日本、美国、俄罗斯、印度、马来西亚、韩国等；按功能分有：实用型、教学型、工艺型、喜庆型、专用型等。

这30多件洋算盘虽不能涵盖世界各国算盘的全貌，但它是演绎异域经济、科技、文化创造力与人文风情的橱窗，更是中华文化开放性的直接见证。

欣赏这些外国算盘，让您跨越时空，感悟人类文明共建共享共赢的境界。

品评这些外国算盘，与您建构、解读中外算盘文化交流源远流长的空间。

▲日本·一四菱珠7档插笔文具板算盘
Japan · 1—4 rhombus beads, 7 rods, stationery abacus with pen hole

▲日本·一五菱珠15档拱形座底算盘
Japan·1—5 rhombus beads，15 rods，arched abacus with seatboard

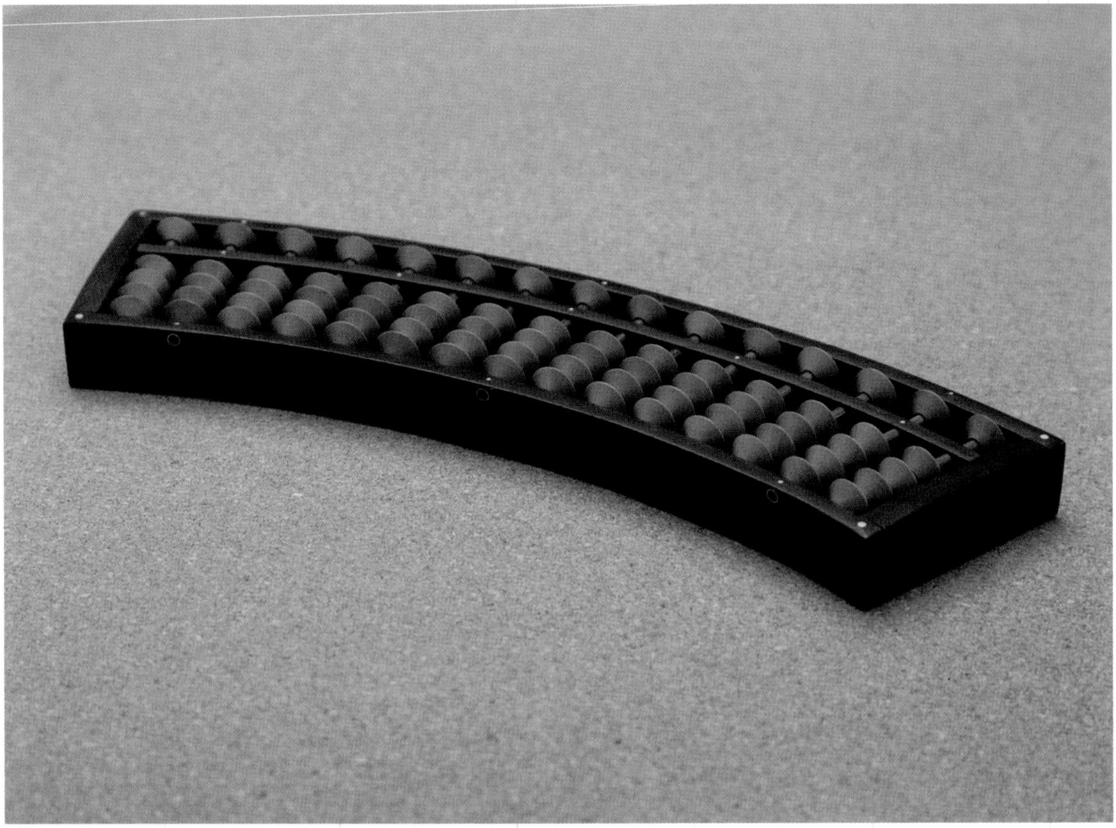

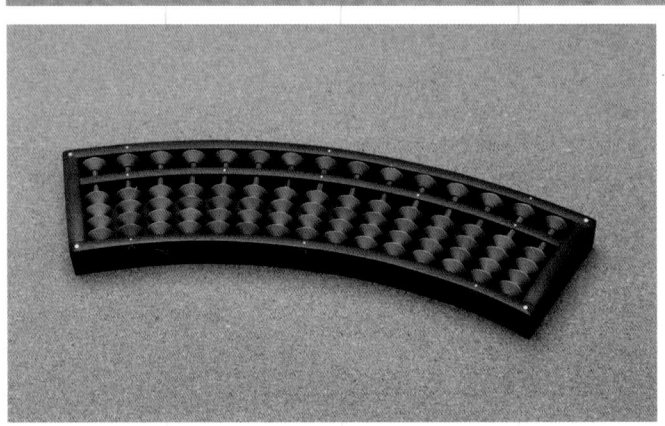

▲日本・一四菱珠15档扇形算盘
Japan・1—4 rhombus beads，15 rods，fan—shaped abacus

▲日本 · 形态迥异的算盘　Japan · varied abacus

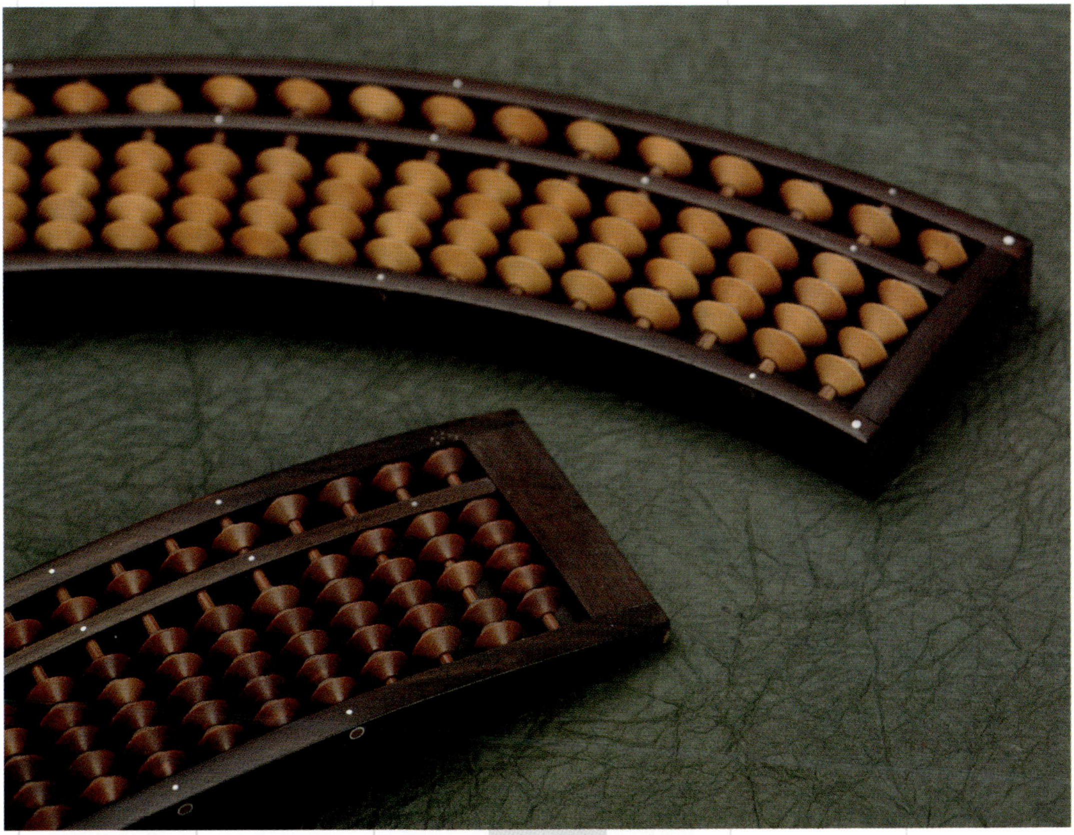

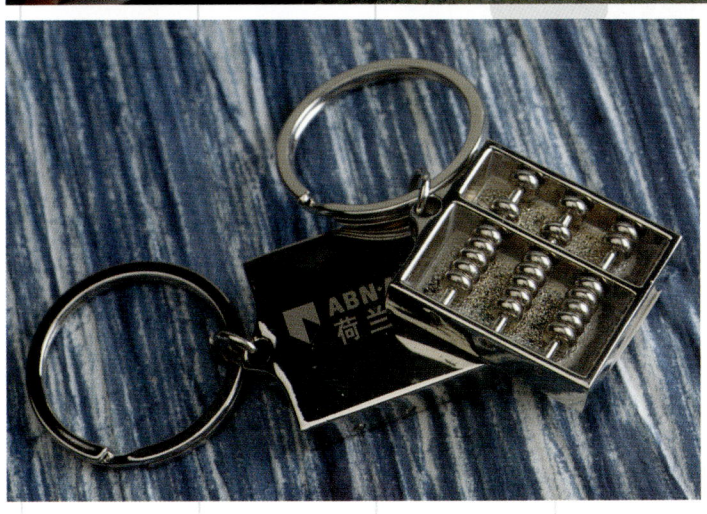

荷兰 · 二五圆珠3档钥匙圈吊饰不锈钢算盘
Holland · 2–5 round beads, 3 rods, stainless steel key ring abacus

▲日本·一四鼓珠12档计时算盘
Japan·1—4 drum beads，12 rods，timer abacus

▲日本·一四菱珠21档腰带算盘
Japan · 1—4 rhombus beads, 21 rods,belt abacus

▲日本·多功能算盘
Japan · multifunctional abacus

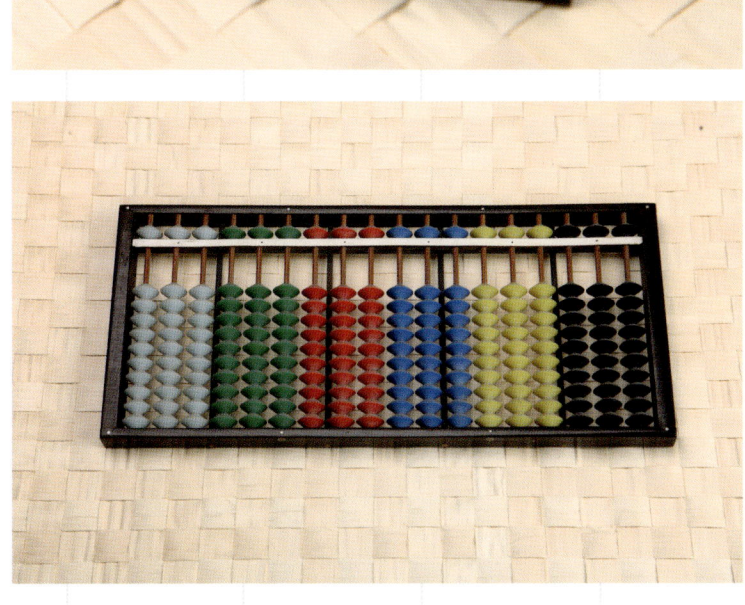

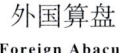
▲美国·一十菱珠18档彩色算盘
U.S.·1—10 rhombus beads,
18 rods,multicolor abacus

137

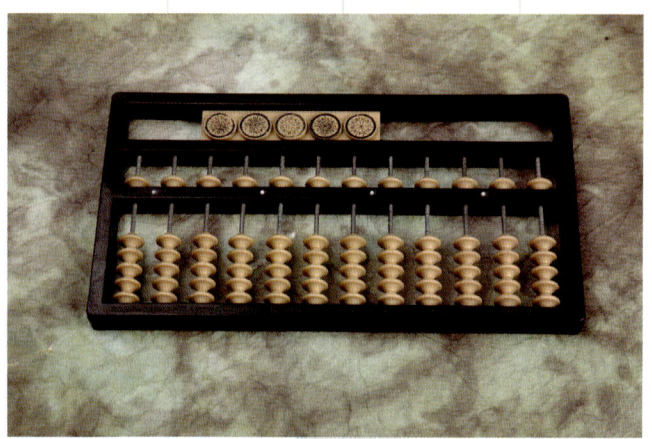

▲马来西亚·一五碟珠12档双梁算盘
Malaysia · 1—5 dish beads, 12 rods, double beams abacus

▲俄罗斯·十圆珠8档双色斜坡式算盘
Russia · 10 round beads , 8 rods , two colour slop abacus

▲印度·二五菱珠11档彩色串吊式算盘
India · 2—5 rhombus beads，11 rods，colourful，bunched abacus

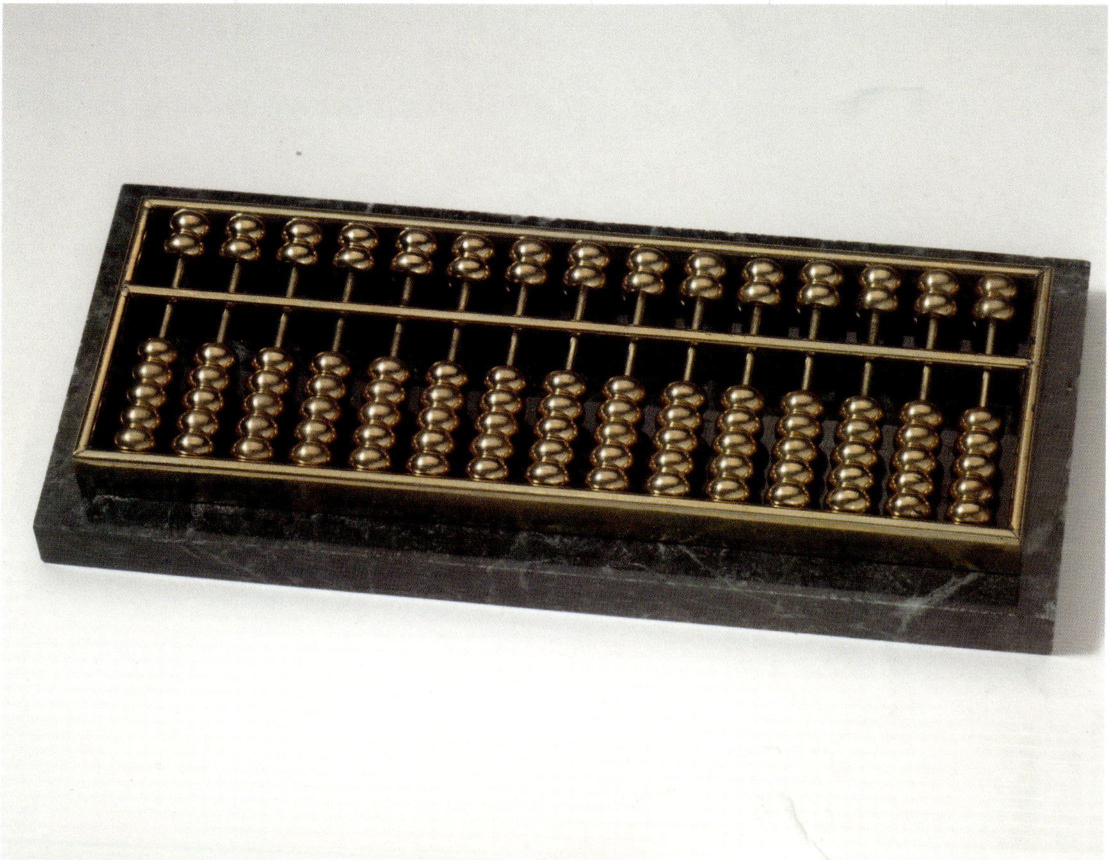

美国 · 二五圆珠15档礼品镀金算盘
U.S. · 2—5 round beads,15 rods, gold—plating gift abacus

日本·一四碟珠3档座式算盘
Japan · 1—4 dish beads, 3 rods, stand abacus

日本 · 二十菱珠15档算盘
Japan · 2—10 rhombus beads, 15 rods, abacus

日本·十菱珠无梁彩色儿童算盘
Japan · 10 rhombus beads, no rods, colourful abacus for child

日本·手执算盘的仕女及儿童陶泥像
Japan · maidservant and child with abacus in hands

日本·一四菱珠11档喜合式算盘和储蓄柜
算盘
Japan·1—4 rhombus beads, 11 rods,
well—formed abacus and drawer abacus

日本·众多类型计算器算盘
Japan·varied types of calculator abacus

日本·一四菱珠23档清盘器算盘
Japan · 1—4 rhombus beads, 23 rods, winding—up abacus

日本·一四菱珠22档折叠式算盘
Japan·1—4 rhombus beads,22 rods,folding abacus

日本·彩色儿童算盘与印有算珠图案的扑克牌(珠算扑克牌)
Japan·children's colourful poker with abacus on it (abacus poker)

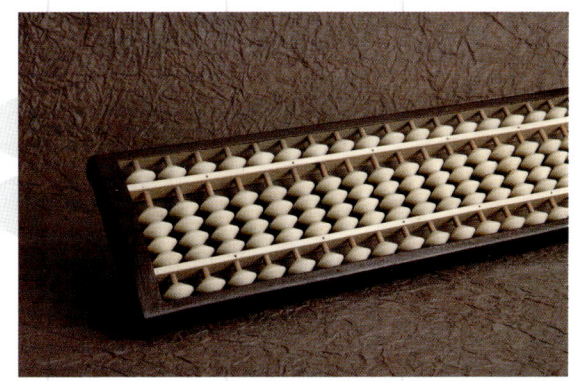

日本·一四一菱珠23档负数算盘
Japan · 1—4—1 rhombus beads, 23 rods, negative number abacus

日本 · 一四半菱珠17档半珠式盲人算盘
Japan · 1—4 half rhombus beads, 17 rods, half beams abacus for the sightless

日本·趣味风铃算盘　Japan·funny windbell abacus

日本·花猫与算盘吊饰　Japan·cat and abacus pendant

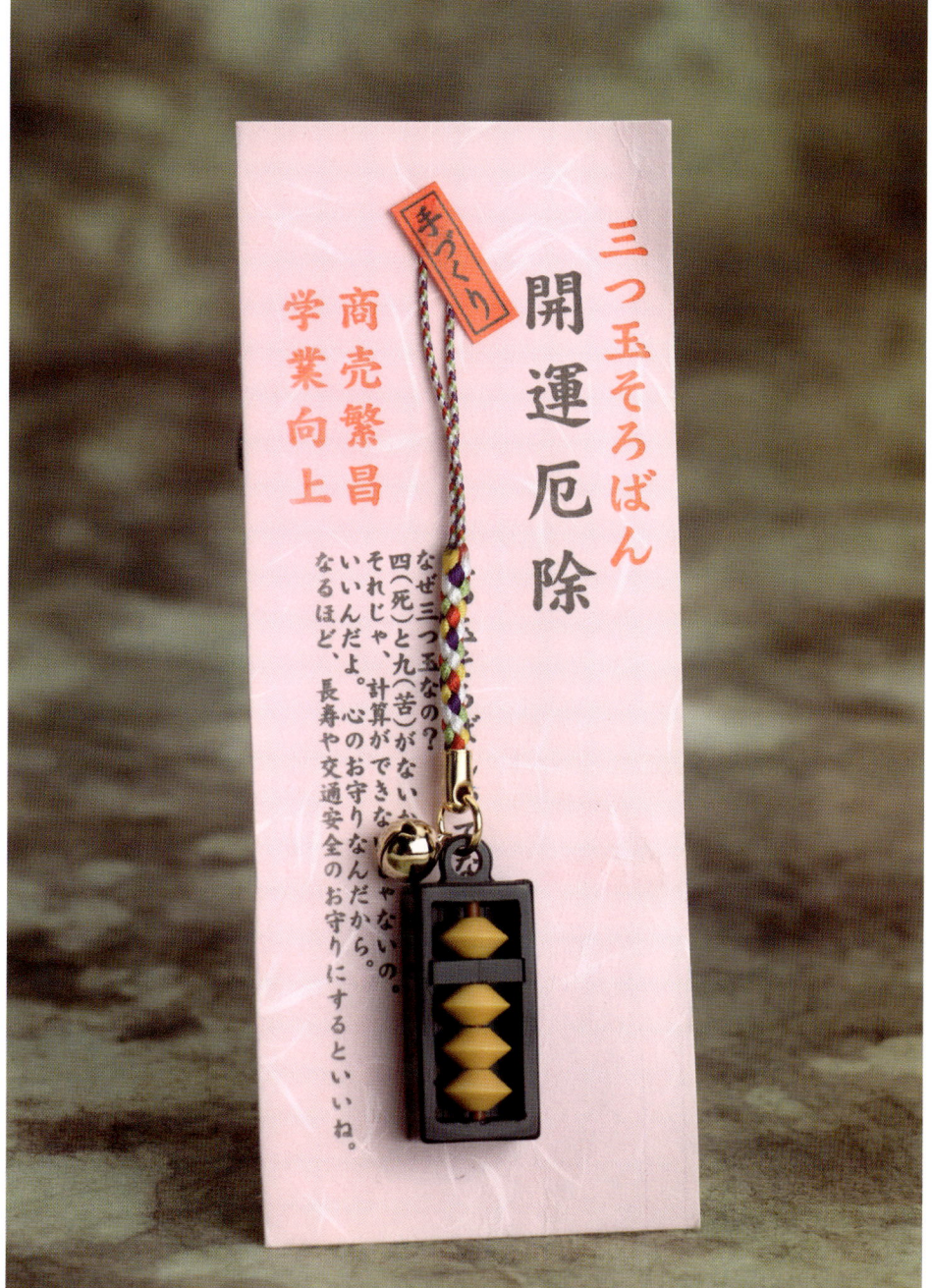

なぜ三つ玉なの？四（死）と九（苦）がないから、計算ができないじゃないの。それじゃ、計算ができないんだよ。心のお守りなんだから。いいんだよ。心のお守りなんだから。なるほど、長寿や交通安全のお守りにするといいね。

三つ玉そろばん
開運厄除
手づくり
商売繁昌
学業向上

日本・开运厄除吉祥算盘　　Japan・paustika and lucky abacus

美国·二五鼓珠9档礼品镀金算盘
U.S. · 2—5 drum beads,9 rods,gold—plating gift abacus

韩国·钥匙圈吊饰不锈钢算盘　Korea·stainless steel key ring abacus

图书在版编目（ＣＩＰ）数据

算盘珍藏：汉英对照 / 陈宝定，陈沅沅著. — 上
海：立信会计出版社，2009.12
ISBN 978-7-5429-2445-2

Ⅰ．①算… Ⅱ．①陈… ②陈… Ⅲ．①算盘－收
藏－汉、英 Ⅳ．①G894

中国版本图书馆CIP数据核字(2010)第018167号

算盘珍藏

出版发行	立信会计出版社		
地　　址	上海市中山西路 2230号	邮政编码	200235
电　　话	（021）64411389	传　　真	（021）64411325
网　　址	www.lixinaph.com	E-mail	lxaph@sh163.net
网上书店	www.shlx.net	Tel：（021）64411071	
经　　销	各地新华书店		

印　　刷	上海精英彩色印务有限公司
开　　本	787豪米 × 1092毫米　1/16
印　　张	10.5
字　　数	5千字
版　　次	2009 年 12 月 第 1 版
印　　次	2010 年 4 月 第 1 次
印　　数	1-3000
书　　号	ISBN 978 - 7 - 5429 - 2445 - 2/G
定　　价	48.00元

如有印订差错，请与本社联系调换